Susan B. Kraat, MLS
Editor

Relationships Between Teaching Faculty and Teaching Librarians

Relationships Between Teaching Faculty and Teaching Librarians has been co-published simultaneously as *The Reference Librarian*, Numbers 89/90 2005.

Pre-publication REVIEWS, COMMENTARIES, EVALUATIONS . . .

"For those new to library instruction, or those who would appreciate a new approach to current practices, THIS BOOK IS A VERY GOOD CHOICE. . . . A UNIQUE COLLECTION of essays showcasing various types of library instruction, supplying successful collaborative undertakings between librarians and faculty, and in turn offering new ways to expand existing collaborative efforts in many academic institutions. As an instructional librarian, I value not only the appendices, which include sample worksheet forms, but also the extensive 'Works Cited' lists attached to each essay."

Marianne B. Eimer, MLS
Head of Reference and Instruction
Daniel A. Reed Library
SUNY Fredonia
Fredonia, New York

The Haworth Information Press®
An Imprint of The Haworth Press, Inc.

Relationships Between Teaching Faculty and Teaching Librarians

Relationships Between Teaching Faculty and Teaching Librarians has been co-published simultaneously as *The Reference Librarian*, Numbers 89/90 2005.

Monographic Separates from *The Reference Librarian*™

For additional information on these and other Haworth Press titles, including descriptions, tables of contents, reviews, and prices, use the QuickSearch catalog at http://www.HaworthPress.com.

Relationships Between Teaching Faculty and Teaching Librarians, edited by Susan B. Kraat, MLS (No. 89/90, 2005). *Documents the efforts of teaching librarians to establish effective communication with teaching faculty.*

Research, Reference Service, and Resources for the Study of Africa, edited by Deborah M. LaFond and Gretchen Walsh (No. 87/88, 2004). *Examines reference services in terms of Africa and libraries in both the United States and Africa.*

Animals Are the Issue: Library Resources on Animal Issues, edited by John M. Kistler, MLS, MDiv (No. 86, 2004). *Contains listings of written and electronic resources that focus on the ethics of animal treatment and use.*

Digital versus Non-Digital Reference: Ask a Librarian Online and Offline, edited by Jessamyn West, MLib (No. 85, 2004). *A librarian's guide to commercial Ask A Librarian (AskA) and tutorial services and how they compare to traditional library services.*

Cooperative Reference: Social Interaction in the Workplace, edited by Celia Hales Mabry, PhD (No. 83/84, 2003). *This informative volume focuses on effective social interactions between library co-workers, presenting perspectives, firsthand accounts, and advice from experienced and successful reference librarians.*

Outreach Services in Academic and Special Libraries, edited by Paul Kelsey, MLIS, and Sigrid Kelsey, MLIS (No. 82, 2003). *Presents an array of models and case studies for creating and implementing outreach services in academic and special library settings.*

Managing the Twenty-First Century Reference Department: Challenges and Prospects, edited by Kwasi Sarkodie-Mensah, PhD (No. 81, 2003). *An up-to-date guide on managing and maintaining a reference department in the twenty-first century.*

Digital Reference Services, edited by Bill Katz, PhD (No. 79/80, 2002/2003). *A clear and concise book explaining developments in electronic technology for reference services and their implications for reference librarians.*

The Image and Role of the Librarian, edited by Wendi Arant, MLS, and Candace R. Benefiel, MA, MLIS (No. 78, 2002). *A unique and insightful examination of how librarians are perceived–and how they perceive themselves.*

Distance Learning: Information Access and Services for Virtual Users, edited by Hemalata Iyer, PhD (No. 77, 2002). *Addresses the challenge of providing Web-based library instructional materials in a time of ever-changing technologies.*

Helping the Difficult Library Patron: New Approaches to Examining and Resolving a Long-Standing and Ongoing Problem, edited by Kwasi Sarkodie-Mensah, PhD (No. 75/76, 2002). *"Finally! A book that fills in the information cracks not covered in library school about the ubiquitous problem patron. Required reading for public service librarians." (Cheryl LaGuardia, MLS, Head of Instructional Services for the Harvard College Library, Cambridge, Massachusetts)*

Evolution in Reference and Information Services: The Impact of the Internet, edited by Di Su, MLS (No. 74, 2001). *Helps you make the most of the changes brought to the profession by the Internet.*

Doing the Work of Reference: Practical Tips for Excelling as a Reference Librarian, edited by Celia Hales Mabry, PhD (No. 72 and 73, 2001). *"An excellent handbook for reference librarians who wish to move from novice to expert. Topical coverage is extensive and is presented by the best guides possible: practicing reference librarians." (Rebecca Watson-Boone, PhD, President, Center for the Study of Information Professionals, Inc.)*

New Technologies and Reference Services, edited by Bill Katz, PhD (No. 71, 2000). *This important book explores developing trends in publishing, information literacy in the reference environment, reference provision in adult basic and community education, searching sessions, outreach programs, locating moving image materials for multimedia development, and much more.*

Reference Services for the Adult Learner: Challenging Issues for the Traditional and Technological Era, edited by Kwasi Sarkodie-Mensah, PhD (No. 69/70, 2000). *Containing research from librarians and adult learners from the United States, Canada, and Australia, this comprehensive guide offers you strategies for teaching adult patrons that will enable them to properly use and easily locate all of the materials in your library.*

Library Outreach, Partnerships, and Distance Education: Reference Librarians at the Gateway, edited by Wendi Arant and Pixey Anne Mosley (No. 67/68, 1999). *Focuses on community outreach in libraries toward a broader public by extending services based on recent developments in information technology.*

From Past-Present to Future-Perfect: A Tribute to Charles A. Bunge and the Challenges of Contemporary Reference Service, edited by Chris D. Ferguson, PhD (No. 66, 1999). *Explore reprints of selected articles by Charles Bunge, bibliographies of his published work, and original articles that draw on Bunge's values and ideas in assessing the present and shaping the future of reference service.*

Reference Services and Media, edited by Martha Merrill, PhD (No. 65, 1999). *Gives you valuable information about various aspects of reference services and media, including changes, planning issues, and the use and impact of new technologies.*

Coming of Age in Reference Services: A Case History of the Washington State University Libraries, edited by Christy Zlatos, MSLS (No. 64, 1999). *A celebration of the perseverance, ingenuity, and talent of the librarians who have served, past and present, at the Holland Library reference desk.*

Document Delivery Services: Contrasting Views, edited by Robin Kinder, MLS (No. 63, 1999). *Reviews the planning and process of implementing document delivery in four university libraries–Miami University, University of Colorado at Denver, University of Montana at Missoula, and Purdue University Libraries.*

The Holocaust: Memories, Research, Reference, edited by Robert Hauptman, PhD, and Susan Hubbs Motin (No. 61/62, 1998). *"A wonderful resource for reference librarians, students, and teachers . . . on how to present this painful, historical event." (Ephraim Kaye, PhD, The International School for Holocaust Studies, Yad Vashem, Jerusalem)*

Electronic Resources: Use and User Behavior, edited by Hemalata Iyer, PhD (No. 60, 1998). *Covers electronic resources and their use in libraries, with emphasis on the Internet and the Geographic Information Systems (GIS).*

Philosophies of Reference Service, edited by Celia Hales Mabry (No. 59, 1997). *"Recommended reading for any manager responsible for managing reference services and hiring reference librarians in any type of library." (Charles R. Anderson, MLS, Associate Director for Public Services, King County Library System, Bellevue, Washington)*

Business Reference Services and Sources: How End Users and Librarians Work Together, edited by Katherine M. Shelfer (No. 58, 1997). *"This is an important collection of papers suitable for all business librarians. . . . Highly recommended!" (Lucy Heckman, MLS, MBA, Business and Economics Reference Librarian, St. John's University, Jamaica, New York)*

Reference Sources on the Internet: Off the Shelf and onto the Web, edited by Karen R. Diaz (No. 57, 1997). *Surf off the library shelves and onto the Internet and cut your research time in half!*

Reference Services for Archives and Manuscripts, edited by Laura B. Cohen (No. 56, 1997). *"Features stimulating and interesting essays on security in archives, ethics in the archival profession, and electronic records." ("The Year's Best Professional Reading" (1998), Library Journal)*

Career Planning and Job Searching in the Information Age, edited by Elizabeth A. Lorenzen, MLS (No. 55, 1996). *"Offers stimulating background for dealing with the issues of technology and service. . . . A reference tool to be looked at often." (The One-Person Library)*

The Roles of Reference Librarians: Today and Tomorrow, edited by Kathleen Low, MLS (No. 54, 1996). *"A great asset to all reference collections. . . . Presents important, valuable information for reference librarians as well as other library users." (Library Times International)*

Relationships Between Teaching Faculty and Teaching Librarians

Susan B. Kraat, MLS
Editor

Relationships Between Teaching Faculty and Teaching Librarians has been co-published simultaneously as *The Reference Librarian*, Numbers 89/90 2005.

The Haworth Information Press®
An Imprint of The Haworth Press, Inc.

New York • London • Victoria (AU)
www.HaworthPress.com

Published by

The Haworth Information Press®, 10 Alice Street, Binghamton, NY 13904-1580 USA

The Haworth Information Press® is an imprint of The Haworth Press, Inc., 10 Alice Street, Binghamton, NY 13904-1580 USA.

Relationships Between Teaching Faculty and Teaching Librarians has been co-published simultaneously as *The Reference Librarian*™, Numbers 89/90 2005.

Cover design by Kerry E. Mack.

Library of Congress Cataloging-in-Publication Data

Relationships between teaching faculty and teaching librarians / Susan B. Kraat, editor.
      p. cm.
      "Relationships Between Teaching Faculty and Teaching Librarians has been co-published simultaneously as The Reference Librarian, Numbers 89/90, 2005."
      Includes bibliographical references and index.
      ISBN-13: 978-0-7890-2572-2 (hc. : alk. paper)
      ISBN-10: 0-7890-2572-8 (hc. : alk. paper)
      ISBN-13: 978-0-7890-2573-9 (pbk. : alk. paper)
      ISBN-10: 0-7890-2573-6 (pbk. : alk. paper)
      1. Information literacy–Study and teaching (Higher) 2. Academic libraries–Relations with faculty and curriculum. 3. Electronic information resource literacy–Study and teaching (Higher) I. Kraat, Susan B. II. Reference librarian.
ZA3075 .R45 2005
028.7'071'173–dc22
                                         2004021156

Indexing, Abstracting & Website/Internet Coverage

This section provides you with a list of major indexing & abstracting services and other tools for bibliographic access. That is to say, each service began covering this periodical during the year noted in the right column. Most Websites which are listed below have indicated that they will either post, disseminate, compile, archive, cite or alert their own Website users with research-based content from this work. (This list is as current as the copyright date of this publication.)

Abstracting, Website/Indexing Coverage . . . . Year When Coverage Began

- *Academic Abstracts/CD-ROM* 1994

- *Academic Search: database of 2,000 selected academic serials,*
  updated monthly: EBSCO Publishing 1996

- *Academic Search Elite (EBSCO)* 1995

- *Academic Search Premier (EBSCO)*
  <http://www.epnet.com/academic/acasearchprem.asp> 1995

- *Business Source Corporate: coverage of nearly 3,350 quality magazines*
  and journals; designed to meet the diverse information needs of corporations;
  EBSCO Publishing <http://www.epnet.com/corporate/bsourcecorp.asp> 1995

- *Computer and Information Systems Abstracts <http://www.csa.com>* 2004

- *Current Cites [Digital Libraries] [Electronic Publishing] [Multimedia*
  & Hypermedia] [Networks & Networking] [General]
  <http://sunsite.berkeley.edu/CurrentCites/> 2000

- *EBSCOhost Electronic Journals Service (EJS)*
  <http://ejournals.ebsco.com> 2001

- *Educational Administration Abstracts (EAA)* 1991

- *ERIC Database (Education Resource Information Center)*
  <http://www.eric.ed.gov> 2004

- *FRANCIS. INIST/CNRS <http://www.inist.fr>* 1983

- *Google <http://www.google.com>* 2004

- *Google Scholar <http://scholar.google.com>* 2004

- *Handbook of Latin American Studies* 1999

(continued)

(continued)

Special bibliographic notes related to special journal issues (separates) and indexing/abstracting:

- indexing/abstracting services in this list will also cover material in any "separate" that is co-published simultaneously with Haworth's special thematic journal issue or DocuSerial. Indexing/abstracting usually covers material at the article/chapter level.
- monographic co-editions are intended for either non-subscribers or libraries which intend to purchase a second copy for their circulating collections.
- monographic co-editions are reported to all jobbers/wholesalers/approval plans. The source journal is listed as the "series" to assist the prevention of duplicate purchasing in the same manner utilized for books-in-series.
- to facilitate user/access services all indexing/abstracting services are encouraged to utilize the co-indexing entry note indicated at the bottom of the first page of each article/chapter/contribution.
- this is intended to assist a library user of any reference tool (whether print, electronic, online, or CD-ROM) to locate the monographic version if the library has purchased this version but not a subscription to the source journal.
- individual articles/chapters in any Haworth publication are also available through the Haworth Document Delivery Service (HDDS).

Relationships Between Teaching Faculty and Teaching Librarians

CONTENTS

ABOUT THE EDITOR

Susan B. Kraat, MLS, is a reference librarian and the Coordinator of Library Instruction at the Sojourner Truth Library at the State University of New York at New Paltz. She received her MLS from the University at Albany and her BA in Theatre Arts from Indiania University. Her work has been published in *The Reference Librarian*.

IN MEMORIAM

Dr. William (Bill) Katz passed away on September 12, 2004. Dr. Katz was Editor of the Haworth journals *The Acquisitions Librarian* and *The Reference Librarian* as well as *Magazines for Libraries*, *RQ* (the journal of the Reference and Adult Services Division of the American Library Association), and the "Magazines" column in *Library Journal.* In addition to his contributions to library science as an author and editor, he was a much-beloved professor in the School of Information Science and Policy at the State University of New York at Albany and a mentor to many of his former students in their professional lives. His association with The Haworth Press began in 1980 and lasted more than two decades. His steady hand, friendly guidance, and steadfast leadership will be missed by all of us at *The Acquisitions Librarian*, *The Reference Librarian*, and The Haworth Press.

Introduction:
Do You Really Get More Flies
with Honey?

Susan B. Kraat

Which of your teachers do you remember the most? Why do they stand out in your memory? Perhaps they were the ones who saw something in you that you may not have seen. Memorable teachers are generous of spirit, wishing to give you the opportunity to shine, while they remain in the background. Parker Palmer says that "When we listen to good teachers, they urge us to join them in listening to students as well–for the young have much to say about what helps and what hurts in education and the larger world" (Palmer 2002, 311).

Education is the main focus of reference service in today's academic libraries. Librarians teach. They teach a smorgasbord of single-session, course-related, course-integrated, or credit-bearing courses in nearly every discipline. Teaching librarians depend upon communication with faculty to provide a foundation for their class/course/session. They are proud of their proactive efforts to create and sustain meaningful relationships with faculty in disciplines across the board.

In *The Collaborative Imperative: Librarians and Faculty Working Together in the Information Universe*, Dick Raspa and Dane Ward have brought together a fine collection of essays about librarians and faculty working together. Three types of connections that librarians can make

[Haworth co-indexing entry note]: "Introduction: Do You Really Get More Flies with Honey?" Kraat, Susan B. Co-published simultaneously in *The Reference Librarian* (The Haworth Information Press, an imprint of The Haworth Press, Inc.) No. 89/90, 2005, pp. 1-3; and: *Relationships Between Teaching Faculty and Teaching Librarians* (ed: Susan B. Kraat) The Haworth Information Press, an imprint of The Haworth Press, Inc., 2005, pp. 1-3. Single or multiple copies of this article are available for a fee from The Haworth Document Delivery Service [1-800-HAWORTH, 9:00 a.m. - 5:00 p.m. (EST). E-mail address: docdelivery@haworthpress.com].

Digital Object Identifier: 10.1300/J120v43n89_01

with faculty are described by Doug Cook in "Creating Connections": networking (the least formal and probably most common), coordination (requiring some level of communication), and collaboration (the most complex and time-consuming) (Raspa & Ward 2000, 26).

This volume, *Relationships Between Teaching Faculty and Teaching Librarians*, has something for all teaching librarians, from the cynic to the idealist. Several articles address the intricacies of working with faculty at the collaborative level. The experiences of these librarians offer the reader glimpses of some of the BIG issues:

- Assigning Grades
- The Teaching and Learning Environment
- Course Growth and Maintenance
- Time
- Understanding the Student
- Respecting Each Other: Collegiality

There is even a story of teaching an actual course within an academic discipline. "We have learned that developing library instruction cannot be done in isolation. Librarians must go beyond our efforts to define information literacy competencies and to assess library instruction. We must enter into a 'conversation' with faculty about teaching and learning" (McNeill 2003, 8).

Why are librarians so preoccupied with faculty members' perceptions of Information Literacy or Library Instruction or whatever label you care to call it? Terri Holtze writes ". . . it all comes down to the relationship you have with other faculty at your institution" (Holtze 2001, 1). In her poster session presented at the 2001 ACRL Conference, called *50+ Ways to Reach Your Faculty*, she suggested a myriad of approaches to curry favor with faculty members, including everything from sharing coffee to obtaining a second or third degree in a different academic discipline.

The Middle States Commission on Higher Education has mandated that Information Literacy be included as part of a general education requirement. If faculty were not calling you for library instruction before the mandate, they probably are now. Still, librarian Glenna Westwood observes that collegiality can have limits: "I no longer complain that some of my teaching colleagues do not take me seriously or treat me as a professional. If you attend enough meetings where faculty treat each other with disrespect, you understand that some faculty act this way toward everyone, not just toward librarians" (Chiste 2000, 204).

Librarian/faculty relationships are critical to the success or failure of library instruction. A wise administrator once said to me, "This sort of program will prosper or not, mainly because of the wishes of the faculty." As 21st century reference librarians, we can learn from the collected tales of our colleagues' efforts in and out of the classroom.

REFERENCES

Chiste, Katherine Beaty, Andrea Glover, and Glenna Westwood. 2000. Infiltration and Entrenchment: Capturing and Securing Information Literacy Territory in Academe. *The Journal of Academic Librarianship* 26, no. 3, 202-208. Wilson Select Plus (4 April 2002).

Holtze, Terri L. *50+ Ways to Reach Your Faculty*, poster session presented at the Association of College & Research Libraries Conference. Denver: March 17, 2001.

McNeill, Kitty and Beth Haines. 2003. Scholarship of Teaching and Librarians: Building Successful Partnerships with Faculty. *Georgia Library Quarterly* 39, no. 4, Winter. Wilson SelectPlus (28 July 2003).

Palmer, Parker. 2002. Afterword: What I Heard Them Say. In *Stories of the Courage to Teach*, edited by Sam M. Intrator. San Francisco: Jossey-Bass.

Raspa, Dick and Dane Ward. 2000. *The Collaborative Imperative: Librarians and Faculty Working Together in the Information Universe*. Chicago: American Library Association.

"Getting Psyched"
About Information Literacy:
A Successful
Faculty-Librarian Collaboration
for Educational Psychology and Counseling

Lynn Lampert

SUMMARY. Librarians and Educational Psychology and Counseling faculty in the Michael D. Eisner College of Education at California State University Northridge are collaborating to design instructional sessions with assessment components to support newly adopted department information competence goals and curricula. This current collaboration between librarians, faculty, and departmental administrators offers a model for incorporating information literacy instruction into pre-service programs for future educators, counselors, and administrators. Through funding from a California State University Information Competence grant, faculty have identified three information literacy competency skill sets (Basic, Research, and Professional/Field competencies) that now comprise a part of the department's new learning outcomes for

Lynn Lampert is Senior Assistant Librarian and Coordinator of Information Literacy, California State University Northridge, Oviatt Library, 18111 Nordhoff Street, Northridge, CA 91330-8327 (E-mail: lynn.lampert@csun.edu).

[Haworth co-indexing entry note]: "'Getting Psyched' About Information Literacy: A Successful Faculty-Librarian Collaboration for Educational Psychology and Counseling." Lampert, Lynn. Co-published simultaneously in *The Reference Librarian* (The Haworth Information Press, an imprint of The Haworth Press, Inc.) No. 89/90, 2005, pp. 5-23; and: *Relationships Between Teaching Faculty and Teaching Librarians* (ed: Susan B. Kraat) The Haworth Information Press, an imprint of The Haworth Press, Inc., 2005, pp. 5-23. Single or multiple copies of this article are available for a fee from The Haworth Document Delivery Service [1-800-HAWORTH, 9:00 a.m. - 5:00 p.m. (EST). E-mail address: docdelivery@haworthpress.com].

graduate students in Educational Psychology and Counseling, making information competence a required learning outcome for the degree program. A description of the dynamic faculty-librarian collaborative process that integrated information literacy instruction and assessment into Educational Psychology 602 (Research Principles) is provided, along with information about the grant and interactions that fostered the development and implementation of this successful graduate student information literacy program. *[Article copies available for a fee from The Haworth Document Delivery Service: 1-800-HAWORTH. E-mail address: <docdelivery@haworthpress.com> Website: <http://www.HaworthPress.com> © 2005 by The Haworth Press, Inc. All rights reserved.]*

KEYWORDS. Counseling, educational psychology, collaboration, information literacy, literature reviews, assessment, information competence, graduate students, Gestalt, subject based competencies, faculty, skill competencies, grant, California State University

In a 1971 *American Psychologist* essay entitled "How Do You Get Those References for That Review Paper?" author Erik Peper offers instructional guidelines and detailed resource based recommendations for training students to face what he identifies as the "one universal problem within graduate education, especially for naïve first-year students, . . . the need to acquire references needed to review the literature" (Peper, 1971, 740). Today's graduate student contends with a much wider array of both general and subject specific resources than those outlined by Peper when conducting a thorough literature review search. Acknowledging that the emergence of the Internet and the proliferation of information resources have led to increased graduate student frustration and research anxiety, Educational Psychology and Counseling (EPC) and library faculty at California State University Northridge are working to provide graduate students with integrated curriculum information literacy training throughout their studies. Through grant funding, EPC faculty elected to incorporate information literacy skills in the department's student learning outcomes, so that student information competence gained acceptance as a required learning outcome for the degree program. The acquisition of EPC information literacy skills will enable students to successfully conduct "the type of research necessary for a thesis of master's degree quality while fostering life-long professional skills to help students deal competently with information through thinking and reasoning" (Mitchell, 2002, 2).

When the current lack of entry-level graduate student information literacy skills is combined with the paucity of higher cognitive skills often displayed in student writing of literature reviews, the critical need for collaboration between librarians and discipline faculty becomes clear. This situation calls for the incorporation of information literacy skills training into graduate curriculum. Unfortunately, specific recommendations and successful strategies for infusing subject specific information literacy skills into graduate studies are not prevalent in information literacy literature. Most cases described in library science literature and guidelines published by associations focus on undergraduate students and programs. However, graduate students are clearly in need of information literacy skills building opportunities–especially through programs that target discipline specific information resources and retrieval skills. This article discusses the dynamic faculty-librarian collaborative process at California State University Northridge that integrated discipline specific information literacy skills instruction and assessment into the campus's graduate program in Educational Psychology and Counseling. In addition to describing the development of subject specific competencies and an information literacy library instruction curriculum for EPC 602 (Research Principles), information about the grant and the faculty-librarian collaborative efforts that fostered the development and implementation of this successful graduate level information literacy program will be discussed.

THE ROADMAP TO COLLABORATION
BETWEEN DISCIPLINE AND LIBRARY FACULTY

The California State University system began the process of developing a programmatic approach to improving the information literacy skills of all students in the early 1990s. Through the creation of the CSU Information Competence Work Group, made up of university and library administrators, librarians, and faculty, successful initiatives were developed to raise awareness for the need for information literacy training in the CSU system. These initiatives aimed to garner support and foster a collective understanding of information literacy by providing definitions, standards, assessment practices and proactive strategies for encouraging information literacy programs on all the CSU campuses. Promoting interest in information literacy programs amongst both librarians and discipline faculty required offering system-wide support through the funding of CSU Information Competence Grants.

As Susan Curzon (2000) notes, "While the CSU libraries have robust bibliographic instruction programs, there had never been external support to develop programs on information competence. Moreover, information competence was mostly the domain of librarians with few college faculty involved" (Curzon, 2000, 485). The CSU Information Competence Grant initiative enabled faculty from all over the CSU system to apply to obtain funding to work on an information literacy project on their campus.

In 2001, faculty in the Educational Psychology and Counseling department at CSUN received one of the first graduate student focused CSU Information Competence Grants. The department's goal as stated in their grant proposal was to "incorporate the skills of information competence in the department's student learning outcomes, so that information competence is a required learning outcome for the degree program" (Mitchell, 2001, 2). Concerned with the quality of student master's theses, writing and research, the department identified two main approaches to work to ensure information literacy in EPC graduate students. The first approach targeted entering EPC graduate students who needed to demonstrate basic information and technology competencies in the required course EPC 451 (Fundamentals of Counseling and Guidance) before they can be admitted to the formal program. The second approach called for the integration of the ACRL Information Literacy Competency Standards for Higher Education (ACRL, 2000) into the core research classes EPC 602 (Research Principles). EPC planned to use general information literacy competency standards like ACRL's and the CSU's (1997) as models to develop modified discipline specific information literacy learning outcomes. Through the grant, the department also wanted to assess graduate students' demonstrated information literacy skill level at several critical junctures in the program before students move on to the culminating phase of their graduate work with their master's thesis or project (Mitchell, 2001).

THEORY vs. PRACTICE–
DEVELOPING DISCIPLINE BASED
INFORMATION LITERACY COMPETENCIES
FOR COUNSELING STUDENTS

Recognizing the need to relate information literacy skills to their specific discipline, selected faculty of the EPC department worked to identify general information and subject based literacy competencies for their graduate students. As one of six departments in the Michael D. Eisner College of Education, EPC has one of the largest enrollments of graduate students on campus. With a wide course of study available within one department, the EPC department reaches a wide range of graduate students with varying interests. The department offers several degree programs leading to the Master of Science in Counseling including: Career Counseling; College Counseling and Student Services; Marriage and Family Therapy; School Counseling; School Psychology and Genetic Counseling. Students choosing to obtain a Master of Arts in Education may either enter the Early Childhood Education or Development, Learning and Instruction programs. A Post-Master's Certificate is also offered in the following areas: Career Counseling; College Counseling and Student Services; Parent-Child Consultation. Many students also participate in the department's California Credential Program in School Counseling and School Psychology. "In Fall 2000 the department's 350 graduate students working towards the Master of Science in Counseling and the Master of Arts in Education, constituted 11% of the total graduate student population at the California State University Northridge campus" (Mitchell, 2001, 1).

In their future careers, students will undoubtedly be forced to continue to contend with the exponential growth of information and information resources that will relate to their workplaces those they counsel and teach. Whether students matriculate to doctoral programs or careers in private practice or public service, as counselors, marriage and family therapists, school counselors, or school administrators, the department expects them to "think critically and engage in reflective, ethical, and legal practice throughout their education and professional lives" (EPC, 2003). Many accreditation agencies have developed guidelines for higher education institutions to implement information literacy programs and assess the students' learning outcomes. As Gary Thompson (2002) maintains, these accreditation recommendations often serve as very powerful motivators for faculty engagement in the collaborative process of integrating information literacy into discipline curriculum. EPC and departments like it nationwide are following closely the actions and recommendations of accrediting agencies and professional associations such as the Council for Accreditation of Counseling and Related Education Program (CACREP, 2001) and the Association for Counselor Education and Supervision (ACES). These organizations are working to incorporate the latest professional competencies into counselor education programs. With ACES' development and endorsement of technology competencies and The National Career Development Association's

(NCDA) adoption of guidelines on career counseling and the Internet, it is clear that both current and future students need to acquire information literacy skills that will develop both their technology and research based skills. As Myers and Gibson (2000) contend, the previous need for pre-service preparation for technology and information based competencies for future counselors and counselor educators is now a requirement for the future and current professionals using the Internet and related research technologies.

THE CURRICULUM PLANNING PROCESS

Before working directly with library faculty, members of the EPC faculty gathered at a grant funded retreat to focus on information literacy and how it could become a departmental learning outcome for their students. At this retreat, faculty explored the types of assignments that might foster student information competence and worked to identify where identified competencies and related assignments could be placed in the curriculum. Faculty also looked at ways they could further develop their own information competence skills. Following the retreat, the faculty studied information competence skills developed by several sources along with other existing models. The department's Information Competence Committee (ICC) developed a model that strategically infused information literacy skills into the curriculum along with three draft competencies: Basic Skills, Research Skills, and Professional Skills. The department's independent work on information literacy curriculum development cemented their collected understanding of their desired learning outcome goals and their understanding of what an information literate EPC graduate student should know.

Following ICC recommendations, which were approved by the EPC department, incoming students are expected to enter the program with Basic Skills Competencies and then progressively attain both Research and Professional competencies during their course of study. The department's Basic Skills Competencies-are defined as the current prerequisite skills that incoming students should possess before admittance into the departmental master's degree program. Students in two sections of the department's required prerequisite course EPC 451 (Fundamentals of Counseling and Guidance) were tested for Basic Skill Competencies in the Fall of 2001. In addition to measuring identified student technology based competencies (knowledge of keyboard/mousing, word processing, Windows, e-mail and Web browsers), the instrument also measured student skill levels in library and information retrieval. Using a 3-point Likert scale (1 = little or no skill; 2 = some skill; and 3 = good/strong skill) the 56 student respondents scored an overall mean of 2.130 in 19 skills in 6 library information categories (Table 1).

"Overall the mean of 32 skills in five technology categories (M = 2.6) were higher than the mean of 19 skills in six library information categories (M = 2.130, with the mean of 19 skills in information resource awareness scoring mid-way between the previous two categories (M = 2.46)" (Mitchell, 2002). While the overall results for the Basic Skill Competencies were somewhat expected, there were many areas of considerable concern in the library and information retrieval areas of the survey. These weaknesses in student information literacy skills were targeted during the later development of the Research Competencies to be taught in EPC 602.

A REVIEW OF THE LITERATURE

The library and EPC have always had a strong relationship when it comes to library instruction at California State University Northridge. But like many campuses nationwide, interactions between faculty and librarians usually tended to be limited and focused on short term and thereby limited learning outcomes goals for library instruction sessions. Library lectures often focused on directing students how to use a specific database like ERIC or PsycInfo or giving an overview of APA style format without faculty and librarians collaborating to connect instruction to assignments in terms of content and timing during the semester. Like many institutions, the standard graduate assignment of the literature review continued to cause countless hours of attention, anxiety and frustration on the part of faculty, graduate students and librarians.

While graduate students in counselor education generally are assigned to write comprehensive reviews of existing literature for courses and preparation of theses, little literature exists on how librarians and discipline faculty can collaborate to support curricular or pedagogical methods for improving graduate performance by engaging students in critical thinking about the research process. Darcy Haag Granello comments that while discipline faculty have historically worked to improve graduate student writing, "what seems to be missing in counselor education literature is a formalized, intentional, and well grounded mechanism designed to teach students how to critically evaluate and

TABLE 1. EPC 451 Skills Survey

Data compiled by EPC Department at California State University Northridge	Frequency Distribution			Mean Skill
	1 = Little/ no skill	2 = Some skill	3 = Good/ strong skill	
Information Knowledge:				
36. Describe differences between/ways information is reported	15	25	14	1.98
37. Identify information/data that is available in various formats	16	17	22	2.11
Understanding and Utilizing the CSUN Library & Online Catalog:				
38. Use a computer connected to the Internet to access the CSUN Online Catalog	4	10	42	2.68
39. Use basic Netscape features to access the CSUN online computer catalog	4	14	38	2.61
40. Know how to use Telnet & WebPAC to connect to the CSUN's online catalog	16	22	18	2.04
41. Search for info by using author's name, title, keywords, or Library Congress Heads	7	16	33	2.46
42. Identify parts of a bibliographic record + location & call number of the item	9	15	32	2.41
43. Identify various locations in library where different resources are located	8	22	25	2.31
Periodical Index and Abstract Databases:				
44. Determine difference between general & subject indexes & abstracts	16	22	18	2.04
45. Identify indexes/abstracts that cover broad areas of knowledge + individual areas	16	19	20	2.07
46. Recognize index/abstract DBs may be accessed individually through a networked CD or the CSUN Libraries Homepage, or via a service provider or aggregator	22	26	14	1.87
47. Identify a specific online index/abstract DB that may include information on a particular research topic	16	26	13	1.95
Search of Databases:				
48. Use the CSUN library's homepage to access databases	13	19	23	2.18
49. Use the databases search engine to locate information on a specified topic	13	14	25	2.23
50. Compile a list of resources (mostly periodical articles) located using DBs		17	25	2.12
CSUN Periodical Titles:				
51. Use the CSUN online catalog to ID periodicals owned by the CSUN library	16	16	24	2.14
52. Access the holdings record to ID specific dates owned + various formats/locations of periodicals within the CSUN library	23	15	18	1.91
Interlibrary Loan:				
53. Determine availability of resources that are not owned by CSUN library	27	15	13	1.75
54. Locate an interlibrary loan while online or in print form	29	17	9	1.64
Overall mean of 19 skills in six library information categories above:				**2.13**

Reprinted with permission.

12

synthesize the material they have collected into cognitively advanced reviews of the literature" (Granello, 2001, 293). Granello cites earlier studies by Bem (1995) and Rivard (1994) that show how comprehensive literature reviews "involve more than simply a recitation of information gleaned from other sources" (Granello, 2001, 293). Skill in writing a literature review is often an overlooked indicator of a beginning researcher's level of information literacy. Identifying three typical skill areas of graduate student training, conducting a literature search, learning to read and understand research, and writing in APA format, Granello's research tangentially touches upon the commonalities and instructional themes that librarians and discipline faculty can collaborate on to improve graduate student information literacy and research skills. While Granello's article is not focused on the need for information literacy training for counseling graduate students, her conclusions highlight how the disconnect between library and counselor education in the area of information literacy education has led to a dearth of information and discussion on how to best incorporate information retrieval and critical writing skills into graduate student literature review assignments.

While information literacy training has not been directly identified in counselor education literature, there have been several articles that touch upon how graduate student understanding and execution of the literature review research and writing process can be improved through the incorporation of a library instruction program curriculum. According to Christine Bruce (1994), the diverse levels of student familiarity and comfort with the research process often stem from the varying emphases instructors and curriculum coordinators place on the research process in the standard literature review and other assignments. Bruce's "phenomenographic exploration" of student's conceptions of a literature review, in the context of a model library information skills subject program for graduate students, identifies six common student conceptions of the literature review process. Bruce's "six conceptions" include understanding the literature review research process as: a list, a search, a survey, a vehicle for learning, a research facilitator, and lastly as a report (Bruce, 1994).

The work of Hart (1998) and Gordon (2002) extends Bruce's recommendation that students working on a literature review should be encouraged to creatively engage in exploring, discussing and challenging their own conceptions of the literature review process with supervision that includes interaction with both discipline faculty and librarians. The research of Green and Bowser (2003) represents the most recent and direct examination of the positive potential of the librarian faculty collaborations to improve graduate students' literature review and overall research methods and practices. Their research also takes the collaboration process a step further than prior research by discussing the impact that discipline faculty/librarian collaboration has on off-campus distance graduate students conducting preparatory thesis literature review research.

Library literature focusing on collaboration, accountability and assessment in library instruction efforts has helped to shape thinking about the integration of information literacy into the curriculum. The benefits of collaboration between librarians and discipline faculty on information literacy initiatives have gained wide attention in library literature and beyond. Recent literature (Raspa and Ward, 2000) shows how librarian-faculty interaction leads to increased communication and greater alignment when developing student research assignments that promote information literacy acquisition. The extension of librarian-faculty collaboration into discipline curriculum development (Stein and Lamb, 1998) also has been cited as one of the key factors helping to move library instruction from the bibliographic instruction model to the newer information literacy model of instruction. Research on the assessment of outcome-focused instruction in Psychology (Daugherty and Carter, 1997) supports the contention that collaboration between discipline and library faculty results in positive measurable learning outcomes for students. Building on research that focuses on the social sciences, primarily in Education and Psychology (Tierno and Lee, 1983; Baxter, 1986), Daugherty and Carter promote the use of assessment to measure the future successes of outcome-focused library instruction that involves the collaboration of librarians and discipline faculty.

Instruction librarians have always placed a great deal of importance on understanding as much as possible about their assigned disciplines and departments. Looking at user information-seeking behavior, as well as citation and communication patterns, gives librarians a better understanding of what areas to emphasize in library instruction sessions. Lyn Thaxton's (2002, 1985) research examines how Psychology faculty, like many other discipline faculty, often overestimate student ability to conduct searches in appropriate databases and evaluate retrieved information. In his article entitled "Information Dissemination and Library Instruction in Psychology Revisited: 'Plus ça Change . . . ,' Thaxton (2002) maintains that the adoption of information literacy acquisition models such as Bruce's (1997) "seven stages of information literacy" may provide the much needed framework for effectively incorporating assignments that affect student critical thinking in relation to required information retrieval exercises in Psychology and beyond.

DEVELOPING A FRAMEWORK FOR EPC INFORMATION LITERACY CURRICULUM INTEGRATION

In an attempt to create an information literacy program that truly develops student information literacy skills for lifelong learning, EPC and librarians worked to create outcomes based competencies that did not become absorbed with the discrete instructional elements and components needed for achieving student success. The process that was ultimately adopted is best described as a Gestalt model for approaching information literacy instruction (Table 2).

Through the process of integrating Information Competence into the learning outcomes for EPC students it became clear that information competence acquisition would involve student attainment of the following individual competencies: Tool Competence, Resource Competence, Research Competence, Social Structure Competence, Publishing Competence and Professional Competence. But Information Competence acquisition as a whole is not any one of those competencies alone–it is

TABLE 2. The Gestalt Model of Information Literacy Acquisition (Mitchell et al., 2003)

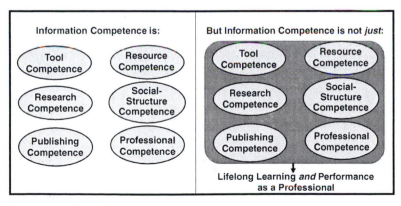

Reprinted with permission.

the instructional grouping of these competencies that yields to the outcome of lifelong learning and performance as a professional (Mitchell et al., 2003).

Under previously used bibliographic instruction models, librarians typically trained EPC graduate students in how to use individual information retrieval tools to gather sources for their comprehensive literature reviews. The emphasis of instruction tended to focus solely on discrete tools deemed critical to the discipline rather than the total process and intellectual interaction that the students would later have with retrieved sources. With the transition from the BI to Information Literacy model of library instruction, librarians are now ready to move beyond resource based library skills training to working to incorporate critical thinking skills into graduate instruction to help raise cognitive writing skills and the ability to evaluate resources for lifelong learning. As Ann Grafstein notes in *A Discipline-Based Approach to Information Literacy*, "Understood this way, IL–as opposed to library or BI–is not restricted to library instruction resources or holdings; . . . it extends beyond the ability to locate information simply to include the ability to understand it, evaluate it, and use it properly" (Grafstein, 2000, 198). Grafstein goes on to point out the limitations in the way that many librarians approach IL instruction with or without faculty collaboration. When approaching information literacy instructional opportunities she writes, "Critical thinking skills and the capacity for lifelong learning are not viewed as skills that are related to specific disciplines, but rather are seen as applying to information seeking generally, independent of any particular discipline or endeavor" (Grafstein, 2002, 198).

The integration of information competencies into a discipline and its learning objectives provides a critical framework for providing the necessary environment and context for the acquisition of information literacy under a Gestalt model information literacy curriculum infusion model. As Thompson and Cronjé (2001) maintain, "Information literacy acquisition is a dynamic process in which there are three factors which influence the process: cognitive space, subject knowledge and access. . . . Each of these elements plays a significant role . . . and cannot function or be in place without the other. Subject knowledge is influenced by cognitive space, which in turn is influenced by access and vice versa" (Thompson and Cronjé, 2001, 4).

With the approved EPC Research Competencies, students are expected to demonstrate some of the following skills: the ability to apply standards to determine timeliness and reliability of information; prepare a search strategy; identify keywords, synonyms and related terms; utilize search techniques (Boolean, proximity, truncation, etc.); determine and execute searches in appropriate databases and indexes; use the Internet as a research tool; understand the Internet in contrast to traditional electronic databases; learn appropriate forms of citations–APA; be able to identify appropriate types of information resources, both print and electronic, for EPC research (EPC, 2001). Utilizing these desired department learning outcomes for EPC Research Competencies, librarians then worked to design effective library instruction sessions to help students acquire these competencies in concert with their assigned coursework.

As the coordinator of information literacy, I assembled a team of four instruction librarians to develop outlines and aligned learning outcomes for the three separate sessions that were scheduled to be three hours in length. The team consisted of librarians assigned to education, psychology and the social sciences. The EPC 602 faculty course mentor provided librarians with a course prototype that included a model syllabus and assignments adopted by the faculty teaching the research course. Librarians worked with the EPC Research Competencies and outlined session learning objectives based on many of the recommendations made in the "Library and Information Resource Instruction for Psychology–Guidelines" (Merriam, La Baugh & Butterfield, 1995). When the outline and proposed content of the three library sessions was complete, librarians and scheduled Fall 2002 EPC 602 faculty met to discuss the class, guidelines and ideas. At this meeting, attended by librarians and EPC faculty and administrators, it was decided that EPC 602 students would complete a survey to determine their comfort level with identified resources before the first library instruction session. The assessment results later helped shape the curriculum of the three sessions and the pace of instruction. As many students expressed lack of comfort and skill level with ERIC, PsycInfo, the library catalog, and Interlibrary Loan, it was clear that the three sessions would primarily focus on these resources with a heavy emphasis placed on hands-on practice time. It was decided that the first session would introduce the EPC graduate students to information about key library resources (catalog, databases), off-campus services (proxy server access, document delivery) and important concepts needed for effective online searching (Boolean logic, truncation, etc.). Students also received instruction on how to retrieve articles from both general subscription citation and full text article databases such as InfoTrac and EbscoHost. Through exercises and class assignments, students reviewed key concepts that would inform their future evaluations of retrieved resources. For example, in one section of

EPC 602, students were asked to locate citations and determine whether or not the citation came from a peer reviewed/scholarly source or a trade journal.

In the second session, students continued to explore the differences between subject and keyword searching. As class assignments were geared toward topic selection for literature reviews, by the second session students were also introduced to available print and electronic thesauri for ERIC and PsycInfo. Students in some sections were assigned to identify descriptors that were related to their proposed research topic by using both the thesauri. Students quickly picked up on the value of the thesauri and the need to determine a list of descriptors and terms to search for their research topic. By the third session, students in all sections of EPC 602 had submitted drafts of their literature reviews or research proposals. EPC faculty had returned the papers and reviewed areas where citations were either inappropriate or missing. Students spent the remainder of the third session lab time locating pertinent citations and research to substantiate their papers. In essence, the content of the third library session became a research lab where students could begin to fine tune their newly found information retrieval skills and relate their findings to the theories of their discipline and course content. During this final session, students received a lot of hands-on time in library instruction labs with one-on-one roving consultation available from both librarians. During this session students also received instruction on document delivery services and APA citation style guidelines. The results of the pre- and post-instruction self-assessment of EPC 602 indicate that students gained an increased amount of comfort and confidence with department identified resources and information competence skills. EPC faculty and librarians were particularly pleased with the increases seen in student comfort with ERIC and PsycInfo (Table 3).

With a group of students varying in age, undergraduate degree background and career experience, these three separate sessions gave librarians and faculty a chance to test out how the newly adopted EPC Research Competencies improved student research skills and projects.

The next step in the integration of information literacy into EPC curriculum calls for discipline faculty and librarians to identify additional classes where the Professional Competencies can be effectively integrated into course curriculum. The Professional Competencies already developed by EPC, call for students to be able to demonstrate the following skills: the ability to use electronic resources in the field; the ability to use school/clinic database management systems in support services, teaching and learning; the ability to conduct research in the

TABLE 3. EPC 602 Surveys

Data compiled by Library California State University Northridge	Likert Scale Measuring Student Self-Reported Level of Comfort (1 = very uncomfortable, 2 = uncomfortable, 3 = neither comfortable or uncomfortable, 4 = comfortable, 5 = very comfortable)	
Name of Database/Index/Research Skills	Before Instruction Mean	After Instruction Mean
PsycInfo or PsychLit	1.80	4.0
ERIC	1.65	4.33
EbscoHost (Academic Search Elite)	1.73	4.5
InfoTrac Expanded Academic ASAP	1.49	3.25
Medline or PubMed	1.23	3.11
Lexis-Nexis	1.33	2.64
Keyword vs. Subject Heading searching	2.13	3.67
Boolean Logic, i.e., use of AND, OR, NOT	1.62	3.4
Truncation or wildcards	1.31	2.67
Citation formats, i.e, APA, MLA, Chicago, etc.	2.06	3.27
Primary vs. secondary sources	1.92	3.08
Locating periodicals or books in the library	2.45	4.25
Peer-reviewed or refereed vs. popular literature	2.08	3.75
Evaluating an author's expertise/credentials	1.60	2.91
Evaluating the reliability of Internet resources	1.92	3.25

field; the ability to access professional information; the ability to help clients and students search for information via the Internet; and lastly the ability to critically evaluate new trends and their impact on the profession. With many of the Professional Competencies requiring students to delve further into understanding the dissemination of their professional literature and continuing to improve their abilities to retrieve appropriate resources through both subscription and open Internet based resources, librarians and faculty will certainly need to continue collaborating on designing meaningful library instruction sessions that are integrated to coursework.

CONCLUSION

Prior to the awarding of the CSU Information Competence grant, librarians and EPC faculty had traditionally collaborated to bring graduate students into the library to learn about resources, both print and electronic. Instruction was given upon faculty request, largely through an on-demand model and sometimes tailored to assignments and applicable resources. The library instruction was not always closely linked to the curriculum in terms of learning outcome goals. Instruction typically consisted of one visit to a library instruction lab. But it is not enough for students to learn discrete resources of information retrieval and formats publication while they are enrolled in pre-service programs. They must be immersed, through assignments and interaction with librarians and discipline faculty, in the totality of all of the information competencies that make their field unique and rewarding. As Sabella and Tyler (2001) argue, while some practicing counselors will maintain that it is viable for them to perform their jobs by "keeping index cards instead of a database; using a typewriter in lieu of a word processor; using overheads in lieu of multimedia presentations; and relying on perhaps a handful of periodicals rather than accessing the highly expansive menu of online full-text resources," professionals who resist acquiring new information literacy skills, regardless of the technological context, will undoubtedly fall further behind the cutting edge trends of their field of study (Sabella and Tyler, 2001, 1).

The Educational Psychology and Counseling department realized that the incorporation of technology and research competencies in graduate student information literacy training would have a tremendous impact both within and beyond required course curriculum. The faculty developed information competencies with the forethought that lifelong learning was a necessary outcome. The discipline faculty then collaborated with the library faculty to create a program that fosters information literacy in its students and faculty. The collaborative factors that continue to make this graduate information literacy program flourish include flexibility, creative curriculum planning, and the active and equal participation of discipline and library faculty. While the institutional support put forth through CSU grant funding cannot be underestimated, the collaborative work of EPC faculty and librarians will continue long after funding evaporates because of the shared planning and added instruction that promotes student information competency acquisition and positively impacts student learning. The independent commitment of EPC faculty to provide assignments and extensive class time for students to actively engage with the research process has allowed students to gain comfort with the department's recommended research competencies. As the program moves forward to tackle proposed EPC Professional Competencies, it will remain imperative for EPC faculty and librarians to continue to meet and maintain open communication and appreciation for how information literacy research enriches both of our disciplines. Continual interaction between librarians and faculty is needed to ensure student success in information retrieval and foster the development of cognitive thinking skills needed to critically evaluate retrieved sources. Infusing information literacy instruction into college and university curriculum takes a long term collaborative commitment on the part of librarians, discipline faculty, and university administrators.

ACKNOWLEDGMENTS

This article about the successful collaboration of librarians and discipline faculty was shaped in so many ways by the support of many colleagues. Special thanks to colleagues in the CSU: Rie Rogers Mitchell, Chair of the EPC Department at California State University Northridge; Merril Simon, Professor in EPC; Gregory Jackson, Professor in EPC; Ilene Rockman, Coordinator of the CSU Information Competence Program; Susan Curzon, Dean of the University Library at CSU Northridge. The author is also grateful to her colleague, Elisabeth Leonard of Wake Forest University, whom she met at ACRL Immersion 2002, for providing continued guidance.

REFERENCES

Association of College and Research Libraries. 2000. *ACRL Information Literacy Competency Standards for Higher Education.* Chicago, IL. Available at http://www.ala.org/Content/NavigationMenu/ACRL/Standards_and_Guidelines/standards.pdf.

Baxter, P.M. 1987. The benefits of inclass bibliographic instruction. *Teaching of Psychology* 13: 40-41.

Bem, D.J. 1995. Writing a review article for *Psychological Bulletin. Psychological Bulletin* 118:172-177.

Bruce, Christine Susan. 1994. Research student's early experience of the dissertation literature review. *Studies in Higher Education* 19(2): 217-230.

_____. 1997. *The Seven faces of Information Literacy.* Adelaide: Auslib Press.

Commission on Learning Resources and Instructional Technology Information Competence Work Group. 1997. *Information Competence in the CSU: A Report Submitted to the Commission on Learning Resources and Instructional Technology.* Available at http://www.calstate.edu/LS/FinalRpt_95.doc (accessed April 18, 2003).

Connor-Greene, P.A. & Greene, D.J. 2002. Science or snake oil? Teaching critical evaluation of "research" reports on the Internet. *Teaching of Psychology* 29(4): 321-324.

Council for Accreditation of Counseling and Related Educational Programs (CACREP). (2001). *The 2001 Standards.* Alexandria, VA. Available at http://www.counseling.org/cacrep/2001standards700.htm (accessed April 18, 2003).

Curzon, Susan. 2000. Developing a program of information literacy: How California State University did it. *College and Research Libraries News* 61(5): 485-491.

Daugherty, Timothy K., Carter, Elizabeth W. 1997. Assessment of outcome-focused library instruction in psychology. *Journal of Instructional Psychology* 24(1): 29-34.

Department of Educational Psychology and Counseling (EPC). 2003. *Student Learning Outcomes* [Department Web Site]. Available at: http://www.csun.edu/EducationalPsychologyAndCounseling/index.html (accessed April 18, 2003).

Department of Educational Psychology and Counseling (EPC). 2001. *Survey of EPC 451(Introduction to Counseling, Fall 2001) regarding basic information competence skills.* Available at: http://www.csun.edu/EducationalPsychologyAndCounseling/ACES/word/document12.doc (accessed April 18, 2003).

Gordon, W.F. and G.D.J. Stewart. 2002. Report on a pilot project: Using a virtual classroom to develop literature review writing skills. *South African Journal of Library and Information Science* 68(1): 68-78.

Grafstein, Ann. 2002. A discipline-based approach to information literacy. *The Journal of Academic Librarianship* 28(4) 197-204.

Granello, Darcy, Haag. 2001. Promoting cognitive complexity in graduate written work: Using Bloom's Taxonomy as a pedagogical tool to improve literature reviews. *Counselor Edcuation and Supervision* 40: 292-307.

Green and Bowser. 2003. Evolution of the thesis literature review: A Faculty-librarian partnership to guide off-campus graduate research and writing. In *Learning to Make a Difference: Proceedings of the 11th National Conference of the Association of College and Research Libraries*, held in Charlotte, North Carolina April 10-13, 2003, edited by Hugh A. Thompson, 245-250. Chicago, IL: Association of College and Research Libraries.

Hart, Chris. 1998. *Doing a Literature Review: Releasing the Social Science Research Imagination.* London: Sage Publications.

Merriam, Joyce, Ross T. LaBaugh, and Nancy E. Butterfield. 1992. Library Instruction for Psychology Majors: Minimum Training Guidelines. Teaching of Psychology 19(1): 34-36.

Mitchell, Rie Rogers, Gregory Jackson, Lynn Lampert and Merril Simon. 2003. *Integrating Information Competence into the Learning Outcomes for Educational Psychology Counseling Students*, a presentation for the CSU Chancellor's Workshop on Information Competence, March 7, 2003. Available at http://library.csun.edu/llampert/EPCpresent327.ppt (accessed April 18, 2003).

Mitchell, Rie Rogers, Gregory Jackson, Merril Simon and Lynn Lampert. 2002. *Future Step in Counselor Education.* [Presentation Summary]. Available at http://www.csun.edu/EducationalPsychologyAndCounseling/ACES/index.html (accessed April 18, 2003).

Mitchell, Rie Rogers. 2002. *Final Report on Information Competence Grant.* Available at: http://www.csun.edu/EducationalPsychologyAndCounseling/ACES/word/document18.doc (accessed April 18, 2003).

_____. 2001. *Ensuring Information Competence in EPC Graduate Students* (Information Competence Grant Proposal). Available at: http://www.csun.edu/EducationalPsychologyAndCounseling/ACES/word/document1.doc (accessed April 18, 2003).

Myers, Jane E. and Donna M. Gibson. 2002. *Technology Competence of Counselor Educators*. Greensboro, NC: ERIC Clearinghouse on Counseling and Student Services, April 18, 2003, ERIC Document Reproduction Service E*Subscribe, ERIC, ED 435947.

Peper, Erik. 1971. How do you get those references into that review paper? *American Psychologist* 26(8): 740-742.

Raspa, Dick and Dane Ward. 2000. *The Collaborative Imperative: Librarians and Faculty Working Together in the Information Universe*. Chicago: American Library Association.

Rivard, L.P. 1994. A review of writing to learn in science: Implications for practice and research. *Journal of Research in Science Technology* 31: 969-983.

Sabella, R.A., & Tyler, J.M. 2001. School counselor technology competencies for the new millennium. In Sandhu, D.S., *Elementary school counseling in the new millennium*. Alexandria, VA: American Counseling Association.

Stein, Linda, and Jane Lamb. 1998. Not just another BI: Faculty-librarian collaboration to guide students through the research process. *Research Strategies* 16(1): 29-39.

Thaxton, Lyn. 2002. Information dissemination and library instruction in psychology revisited: "Plus ça Change. . . ." *Behavioral and Social Sciences Librarian* 21(1): 1-14.

_____. 1985. Dissemination and use of information by psychology faculty and graduate students: Implications for bibliographic instruction. *Research Strategies* 3: 116-24.

Thompson, Gary. 2002. Information Literacy Accreditation Mandates: What They Mean for Faculty and Librarians, *Library Trends* 51(2): 218-241.

Thompson, Jane Elizabeth and Johannes Cronjé. 2001. A dynamic model of information literacy acquisition. *Mousaion* 19, 2: 3-14.

Tierno, M.J. and J.H. Lee. 1983. Developing and evaluating library research skills in Education: A model for course-integrated bibliographic instruction. *RQ* 22: 284-291.

Finding Common Ground:
An Analysis
of Librarians' Expressed Attitudes
Towards Faculty

Lisa M. Given
Heidi Julien

SUMMARY. Information literacy listservs provide opportunities to discuss a range of instruction-related issues. One common theme is librarian-faculty relationships, including positive interactions and complaints. Content analysis is used to investigate librarians' discussions of faculty in BI-L/ILI-L postings from 1995 to 2002. By isolating and anonymizing postings reflecting librarian-faculty relationships and examining these through the authors' experiences as trained librarians and full-time faculty, the paper explores: (1) how librarians frame faculty relationships; and (2) librarians' perceptions of faculty attitudes. The paper concludes with suggestions for transcending unsatisfactory

Lisa M. Given (E-mail: lisa.given@ualberta.ca) is Assistant Professor, and Heidi Julien (E-mail: heidi.julien@ualberta.ca) is Assistant Professor, both at the School of Library and Information Studies, University of Alberta, Edmonton AB, Canada T6G 2J4.

The authors would like to thank research assistants Sandra Anderson, Reegan Breu, and Denis Lacroix for their help on this project.

[Haworth co-indexing entry note]: "Finding Common Ground: An Analysis of Librarians' Expressed Attitudes Towards Faculty." Given, Lisa M., and Heidi Julien. Co-published simultaneously in *The Reference Librarian* (The Haworth Information Press, an imprint of The Haworth Press, Inc.) No. 89/90, 2005, pp. 25-38; and: *Relationships Between Teaching Faculty and Teaching Librarians* (ed: Susan B. Kraat) The Haworth Information Press, an imprint of The Haworth Press, Inc., 2005, pp. 25-38. Single or multiple copies of this article are available for a fee from The Haworth Document Delivery Service [1-800-HAWORTH, 9:00 a.m. - 5:00 p.m. (EST). E-mail address: docdelivery@haworthpress.com].

25

experiences with faculty to forge relationships that benefit those individuals both groups must reach–students. *[Article copies available for a fee from The Haworth Document Delivery Service: 1-800-HAWORTH. E-mail address: <docdelivery@haworthpress.com> Website: <http://www.HaworthPress.com> © 2005 by The Haworth Press, Inc. All rights reserved.]*

KEYWORDS. Information literacy, content analysis, librarians' perceptions, listservs

INTRODUCTION

At universities and colleges, librarians and teaching faculty are increasingly working together to offer students support in building strong academic information literacy (IL) skills. However, forging and maintaining strong working relationships between faculty and librarians is no easy task. Misperceptions about different work roles, as well as misinterpretations of personal motivations related to IL instruction, can hinder the development of productive collaboration. By examining and reassessing beliefs about one another, faculty members and librarians can develop strategies for finding common ground in the instructional environment.

LITERATURE REVIEW

There is an extensive body of literature in library and information studies (LIS) that examines trends in information literacy education. Librarians and LIS scholars have examined professional and theoretical issues involved in guiding individuals in the use of information resources, the design of successful library research projects, and the development of information strategies for lifelong learning. Approaches in the literature address a number of contexts–from public to academic libraries, as well as corporate and other special information centers–and focus on the full range of activities that comprise information literacy instruction (e.g., library tours; database searching sessions; critical evaluations of Web resources). Many of these have been written with the specific goal of sharing IL successes in order to guide others in the development of new programs, in the assessment and revision of existing sessions, in the use of technology, or in the management of other incidental instructional components (e.g., Bodi 1990; Drueke 1992). Many professional and scholarly articles also explore the importance of having key outsiders "buy-in" to the importance of information literacy instruction as one core component to the success of these endeavors (cf. Julien 2000; Julien and Boon 2002). Many articles that address the academic context, in particular, regularly identify the support of teaching faculty as a vital component of successful IL initiatives. Before examining librarian's expressed attitudes and experiences with faculty, it is important to first understand the practical and theoretical contexts surrounding this issue.

Faculty and Librarians' Roles in Information Literacy– A Clear Divide

One of the most prevalent themes discussed in the IL literature is that of the experiential separation between faculty members and academic librarians. Although both groups are engaged, at one level, in pursuing the shared goal of educating undergraduate and graduate students, there are many points of difference that affect the faculty-librarian relationship. Numerous articles portray reference librarians' professional goals (i.e., aiding and teaching students in the effective use of information resources) as being at odds with faculty members' research, teaching, and service work. In these discussions, librarians are placed in a supporting role on campus, as individuals whose primary purpose is to offer support for learning activities, particularly, undergraduate students' information needs (e.g., Farber 1999; Hanson 1993).

At the same time, faculty members are portrayed as sitting outside–yet connected to–the daily activities of the academic library. Here, faculty are discussed primarily in their roles as teachers who set curricula for their students (and by extension, influence librarians' work in supporting students' needs). Hardesty (1999), for example, identifies faculty as "the most important group, outside of librarians, who need to understand and appreciate the educational role of the academic library" (243). However, he notes that a major point of conflict is a faculty culture that privileges research, content and specialization, while undervaluing teaching, process and undergraduate students (244). Hardesty marks faculty members' resistance to building library instruction into their classes as a natural reaction to living under constant time constraints, spending "most of their day doing something for which they have little formal training–teaching" (244), and having a limited exposure to librarians' skills and expertise due to inadequate library support during their own undergraduate or graduate study. While Hardesty

(1999) makes clear that faculty members' actions (or inactions) concerning the library arise more out of ignorance than malevolence (244), other authors are less forgiving, and judge faculty members' inattention to IL as a competition that must be tamed, turf that must be claimed, or as a battle to be won (e.g., Chiste, Glover, and Westwood 2000; Snavely and Cooper 1997).

Other studies of faculty members' attitudes toward the library (and IL, in particular) provide additional context concerning faculty members' perceptions (e.g., Cannon 1994; Gonzales 2001; Leckie 1996; Leckie and Fullerton 1999). In an opinion piece entitled "What I want in a librarian: One new faculty member's perspective," Stahl (1997) puts a very personal face on the issue, noting that faculty members want: proactive involvement from librarians–tempered with an acute sense of when to back off; clear communication about the limitations of librarian support for research activities; to be asked for input on library collection development; and, information on new and useful resources within the library. In a companion piece to this work (entitled "What I want in a faculty member: A reference librarian's perspective"), Larson (1998) compiles her own list of wants and needs: faculty recognition that librarians are in the same business of serving students' needs; clear communication with librarians about what is going on in a course; a basic familiarity with the literature and research tools in the faculty members' field; and, involvement of librarians in the design of course assignments, so that they match available library resources. These two works show, in a very personal fashion, the complex issues and emotions surrounding faculty-librarian working relationships.

Librarians as Advocates for Collaboration with Faculty

Many authors implore librarians to forge stronger, more effective working relationships with faculty, and collaboration in IL instruction is one of the most prevalent solutions offered in the LIS literature. Carlson and Miller (1984), for example, note that involving faculty members in library instruction not only allows librarians to be active participants in the library (beyond simple caretakers of the collection), but "the nature of the courses themselves may change, with more emphasis placed on independent library investigation as an integral part of the course" (484). Much of the current literature advocates this integrated model of faculty-librarian working relationships, and points to the development of formal IL courses and programs within established academic curricula as ideal ways to meet students' needs with full faculty support (e.g., Eliot 1989; Stein and Lamb 1998).

While there are numerous benefits to be gained from collaborative partnerships, many authors also point to the pitfalls of poor relationships–particularly in light of existing problems that must be overcome in order to build effective IL programs. And, as many authors note, the onus is frequently on the librarian to create collaborative partnerships (e.g., Bruce 2001; Chiste, Glover, and Westwood 2000). Some authors see this role as one of faculty development, of teaching faculty about the importance of building the library into courses or assignments, and seeing beyond the library's collections to what librarians can offer students. Cardwell (2001), for example, notes that faculty members often create "problematic" assignments when partnerships with librarians are limited or non-existent; where faculty members fail to take the institution's resources into account when designing assignments, students are left to flounder as they attempt to complete assigned work (258). By forging relationships with faculty–by connecting with them at the reference desk, or conducting one-on-one consultations regarding IL strategies appropriate to their classroom needs–many authors point to the benefits that can be made in the development of IL programs, and in serving students' needs (e.g., Carlson and Miller 1984; Hardesty 1999; Iannuzzi 1998; Ren 2000; Winner 1998).

METHODS

Cardwell (2001) advises librarians to "Subscribe to BI-L [ILI-L], or search its archives . . . An active listserv, BI-L[ILI-L] hosts informative discussions on all types of instruction issues. You will learn about programs, successful and unsuccessful, that have been implemented at other institutions. It is also a place for posting questions and joining in on current discussions" (262). It is the prominence of this listserv among IL professionals that prompted it to be selected as the primary source of data for this study. With approval from the moderator, the archives of the listserv were analyzed using a qualitative content analysis method, for postings that related to librarians' relationships with university and college-level faculty members. The seven-year period from September 1995 to December 2002 was included in the analysis. During that time, in May 2002, the listserv changed its name to ILI-L (reflecting the "information literacy" terminology), and got a new moderator. All the postings to the listserv for the period in question were read, those that related to librarian-faculty relationships were separated out, and then these were inductively coded for apparent themes. To ensure trustworthiness, the qualitative analyses were conducted by two research assistants, and the authors. In addition, the number of postings relating to each major theme were summed to identify broad trends in posting patterns. In the sections that follow, the term "librarian" is used to refer to posters of messages on the listserv; these posters self-identified as having active roles in the development of IL programs and/or the implementation of instructional activities within their libraries.

RESULTS AND DISCUSSION

Quantitative Analyses

Prior to completing qualitative analyses of the postings to BI-L/ILI-L, some quantitative analysis was done to assess the relative interest in particular themes over the seven-year period. Postings marked as relevant to the faculty-librarian relationship theme were totaled by yearly quarter (i.e., January to March, April to June, July to September, October to December). Postings relating to perceptions of faculty (including their personalities, competencies, and roles) were by far the most common, with an average of 28.4 postings per quarter. Postings about librarians themselves were the next most prevalent, with 18.9 postings per quarter. Finally, postings that focused on librarians' beliefs about faculties' perceptions of librarians averaged 4.2 per quarter. These trends held for every quarterly period. Figure 1 shows these trends, and demonstrates that postings were greater in number between October and December in all years, possibly reflecting peak periods of instructional activity for librarians subscribed to the list.

Appropriate Roles for Faculty Members–Librarians' Perspectives

Listserv posters expressed a range of expectations for teaching faculty, from grading library instruction assignments, to dealing with plagiarism, to actively promoting information literacy initiatives. In general, librarians expressed a number of expectations concerning faculty members' roles in information literacy instruction, including:

- Faculty should take on large (even primary) roles in IL instruction;

- Faculty should know library resources, understand the structure of the library and its services, be familiar with library jargon–and be able to teach these things to their students;
- Faculty should prepare feasible assignments that develop basic library skills, foster lifelong learning, provide students with variety, and teach critical thinking; in addition, faculty should teach students such specific skills as: computer literacy; ways to avoid plagiarism; how to distinguish between scholarly and popular journals; and, copyright.

At the same time, several posters recognized that librarians might also learn from the faculty members' wealth of teaching experiences, and apply this knowledge to their own IL instructional strategies; one poster, for example, noted: ". . . we don't get a full sense of what course instructors are up against–the depths of confusion, the short cuts students take, the dynamics of a class as a community. Teaching a course helps us figure those things out and it can really help those students that take it." However, many librarians were adamant in their feelings that within the library, librarians should be in control; for instance, posters seem to agree that library spaces (such as classrooms) should be controlled by the library, not by individual faculty members.

FIGURE 1. Number of Postings Per Category

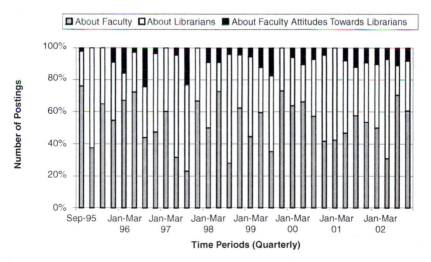

Librarians' Relationships with Faculty Members

Posters also described a variety of efforts to work with faculty, including developing workshops, and liaising with specific departments. However, as one poster noted, "integration and collaboration [with faculty] are slow, painstaking, and include the slippery terrain of being 'polite.'" Some concern was expressed about how faculty conduct themselves during classroom instructional sessions (e.g., marking papers or reading while librarians were speaking; going away to conferences when instructional sessions are scheduled), articulating a theme of "faculty as delinquent children." For example, one poster stated: "the next year she pulled the same thing," as though faculty are trying to "get away" with some sort of bad behavior when they are absent from or complete other work during instructional sessions. Again, these attitudes are not universal, and some comments indicated that librarians at some institutions have experienced consideration from faculty, who typically give them plenty of notice for instructional sessions.

Faculty Members' Attitudes and Competencies– What Librarians Have to Say

One other significant theme on the listserv focused on posters' understandings of faculty members' personalities. Overall, the image constructed was negative. Teaching faculty were represented as:

- possessive and territorial about their class time, course credits, and "their" students;
- inflexible (i.e., not accepting of any course that is not created or taught by themselves);
- rude, "touchy," and generally uncooperative;
- emotionally detached from the teaching role;
- in a "rut" or needing "renewal" in their approaches to classroom activities.

One frequent complaint expressed on the list was that faculty "lack vision" by not understanding that library instruction may require more than one 50-minute session. Various posters suggested that librarians should expect "trouble" from teaching faculty, that some faculty have "inappropriate" or "bad" attitudes, that librarians should expect their requests to be ignored (or "blown off"), and that some faculty need to be "frightened" into "compliance" (by pointing out that familiar library resources are changing or being eliminated). Listserv subscribers were warned not to let themselves be "pushed around" by faculty, so as not to drain librarians' "emotional survival bank." Some posters noted that teaching faculty need to be "tricked" into paying attention to the library, by being cajoled with food and a low pressure environment. Although there were some allowances made for younger faculty, who were characterized as being eager to make a good impression and happy for help with instruction, some posters interpreted this enthusiasm as "laziness," or a sure sign of an instructor trying to "get out of teaching" by letting a librarian run the class. Implicit in these examples is the notion that librarians are dedicated, caring individuals, who continually strive to meet students' needs–despite their frustrations with faculty members' questionable attitudes.

While the vast majority of postings were quite negative in their assessments of faculty members' attitudes, some posters were much more generous in their judgments; positive descriptions referred to faculty members as:

- "reasonable" and "understanding" in terms of IL initiatives;
- having useful knowledge–including expertise regarding students' class-based resource choices;
- in need of a "break"–due to time constraints, research demands and institutional obligations;
- "grateful" for instruction;
- working on a consensus model of decision-making (which can be, at times, at odds with librarians' expectations for quick decisions relating to IL instruction).

One poster suggested that faculty ought to be treated with "care" as any colleague deserves. Although the majority of postings provide negative accounts of faculty-librarian interactions, the minority voices that contradict those images provide a hopeful tone to the discussion; that, in better understanding faculty members' work roles and obligations, librarians may be able to push beyond feelings of frustration and outrage, to find a common ground that will fulfill the goals of most IL programs.

Perceptions of Faculty Members' Opinions of Librarians and Their Work

The listserv postings were filled with assertions about the ways that teaching faculty view librarians and their work. While several posters stated that some teaching faculty are supportive of their library and its goals, most of the perceptions on the part of librarians were less than positive. Many librarians felt that faculty members:

- do not understand librarians' work;
- do not appreciate that librarians often cannot provide instruction on an ad hoc basis, as students need it and wander into the library;
- do not see the intellectual content associated with library instruction;
- view library instruction as only tangential to class content;
- see library use as a set of mechanical skills, requiring only average intelligence to master;
- discount the term "information literacy" as ambiguous, or simply library jargon;
- do not respect librarians.

One poster noted that faculty members view the library as an "obstacle which must be dealt with as quickly and painlessly as possible." Related to this perspective was the point that, "Most faculty seem to view the library as an infrastructural resource and not [as] a learning resource." The bottom line seems to be the perception that faculty do not understand librarians as librarians understand themselves.

How Do Librarians See Themselves?

At the heart of this issue, then, one question remains: How do librarians see themselves in relation to the faculty members on campus? Some posters to the listserv clearly perceived themselves to be full-fledged faculty. Indeed, given the postings that appear on BI-L/ILI-L, it appears that many librarians appreciate being introduced to students as "Professor." By situating themselves as faculty, librarians perceive that they are able to gain credibility in the eyes of students. As one librarian noted: "I NEVER use the word 'serve' when describing what librarians do. I always say 'support' the faculty or the curriculum or student research needs. We facilitate, assist, co-teach, but we do not 'serve' the faculty." While this attitude is clearly empowering for librarians, particularly when trying to connect with students and gain legitimacy in the role of teacher, this approach also (even if unintentionally) places faculty as lesser on the meritorious rungs that define their academic work. Faculty members, for example, typically engage in research and service activities–in addition to their teaching responsibilities–and generally hold doctorate degrees in their areas of specialty. To be equated with librarians, who may not do any research, and who typically hold master's-level degrees, many faculty may rebel and further strive to define themselves as very different from the librarians on campus. By attempting to gain legitimacy by placing themselves as equals, librarians run the risk of further distancing those faculty with whom they need to connect.

Quite a number of criticisms were leveled at librarians by their own colleagues; the result is a clear indication of the complexity of librarians' feelings concerning their relationships with faculty. Some posters expressed frustration with peers who:

- do not want to expand their instructional activities beyond the "traditional";
- are afraid to say no or offend, preferring instead to stick with their perceived public roles as "nice people";
- are unmotivated (often due to feelings of "overwork and techno-stress");
- believe that others see them as on the verge of "extinction" or as "second-class citizens."

Although one poster noted: "The real enemy is in our ranks," another was quick to say: "if we constantly cater to faculty, do things on short notice, etc., then we are complicit in devaluing our own time and efforts." Another stated, "We librarians, along with our colleague professors have failed to instill in our students the joy of real research. We've made the whole process look so stuffy and difficult, or else we've provided so little real help in our one-shot sessions."

There were several points of debate, demonstrating a lack of consensus among librarians about some of these issues. For example, some posters were more sanguine about their status on campus: "We reference/instruction librarians are all handmaidens to the research process, and the term is neither offensive nor pejorative. I have no problem in considering myself a handmaid, or handmaiden, to the teaching faculty. We perform a service, a necessary service, for them; but we aren't their peers even though we may have faculty rank or status." Debate was also evident about whether librarians should train faculty to train students, or train students directly. Additional discussion focused on whether librarians ought to be teaching "computing" literacy, especially word processing.

CONCLUSIONS

The berating of faculty for not being intuitively information literate, or for not taking the time to become information literate is a puzzling attitude–particularly given librarians' professed mandate to guide users and provide instruction in the use of information resources. However, this attitude may also hold the key to understanding the limitations–and complexities–of the librarian-faculty relationship debate. Both explicitly, and by implication of the expressed attitudes explored here, many librarians on the BI-L/ILI-L list made clear that they generally do not consider faculty members to be their clients–only those faculty members' students. The images of troublesome, arrogant faculty, who have little understanding of librarians' roles, point to a problem at the core of the relationship issue: that until librarians embrace faculty as clients themselves, deserving of the same level of respect and support afforded undergraduate and graduate students, IL librarians may continue to fight an uphill battle to bring faculty members onside.

By recognizing that faculty members and librarians are masters of their own (separate, but related) spheres, librarians may make strides in forging respectful and productive working relationships. As well, there are a number of concrete changes that librarians can embrace:

- Try not to presume arrogance, bad intentions, or disrespect on the part of faculty–they are people, just like librarians (or students, or other library clients), and all will have very different attitudes towards librarians and the library;
- Try not to presume that faculty are not committed to IL–or willing to open their classrooms to librarians; they may balk, at first–due to other time constraints or worries about competing institutional agendas–but this does not mean that they are not willing to be involved;
- Try to gain faculty members' trust, by expressing an understanding of their busy lives; offer to provide help with their research or service work, as one way to gain access to their classrooms;
- Recognize that many faculty did not have the benefit of formal library instruction during their own education and have learned to access the world of information in ways that may appear inefficient and ineffective; over the years they have designed personal library-searching systems that work for them–so try to be patient in guiding faculty members in their use of resources, and be proactive in terms of instructional outreach;

- Treat faculty as clients of the library—offer to hold instruction sessions for their research assistants, or offer to set up monthly journal alerts.

All of these suggestions attempt to address a core issue, implicit in the postings examined in this study—respect. Librarians clearly desire it, and faculty members are no different. In order for librarians and faculty to work collaboratively in IL programs, both sides need to find a common ground—ways to speak to one another as colleagues, and also as clients-helpers. If librarians can lay the groundwork for building engaging, productive relationships with faculty by first connecting with them in their roles as researchers—the teaching role will soon follow.

REFERENCES

Bodi, Sonia. 1990. Teaching effectiveness and bibliographic instruction: The relevance of learning styles. *College and Research Libraries* 51, no. 2: 113-119.

Bruce, Christine. 2001. Faculty-librarian partnerships in Australian higher education: Critical dimensions. *Reference Services Review* 29, no. 2: 106-115.

Cannon, Anita. 1994. Faculty survey on library research instruction. *Research Quarterly* 33, no. 4: 524-541.

Cardwell, Catherine. 2001. Faculty: An essential resource for reference librarians. *The Reference Librarian* 73: 253-263.

Carlson, David, & Ruth H. Miller. 1984. Librarians and teaching faculty: Partners in bibliographic instruction. *College and Research Libraries* 45: 483-491.

Chiste, Katherine Beaty, Andrea Glover, and Glenna Westwood. 2000. Infiltration and entrenchment: Capturing and securing information literacy territory in academe. *The Journal of Academic Librarianship* 26, no. 3: 202-208.

Drueke, Jeanetta. 1992. Active learning in the university library instruction classroom. *Research Strategies* 10, no. 2: 77-83.

Eliot, Paula. 1989. The view from square one: Librarian and teaching faculty collaboration on a new interdisciplinary course in world civilizations. *The Reference Librarian* 24: 87-99.

Farber, Evan. 1999. Faculty-librarian cooperation: A personal retrospective. *Reference Services Review* 27, no. 3: 229-234.

Gonzales, Rhonda. 2001. Opinions and experiences of university faculty regarding library research instruction: Results of a Web-based survey at the University of Southern Colorado. *Library and Information Science Research* 18: 191-201.

Hanson, Michelle. 1993. The library as laboratory for interdisciplinary studies. *Teaching English in the Two-Year College* 21: 222-228.

Hardesty, Larry. 1999. Reflections on 25 years of library instruction: Have we made progress? *Reference Services Review* 27, no. 3: 242-246.

Iannuzzi, Patricia. 1998. Faculty development and information literacy: Establishing campus partnerships. *Reference Services Review* 26, no. 3/4: 97-102.

Julien, Heidi. 2000. Information literacy instruction in Canadian academic libraries: Longitudinal trends and international comparisons. *College and Research Libraries* 61, no. 6: 510-523.

Julien, Heidi, and Stuart Boon. 2002. From the front line: Information literacy instruction in Canadian academic libraries. *Reference Services Review* 30, no. 2: 143-149.

Larson, Christine M. 1998. "What I want in a faculty member": A reference librarian's perspective. *Reference and User Services Quarterly* 37, no. 3: 259-261.

Leckie, Gloria J. 1996. Desperately seeking citations: Uncovering faculty assumptions about the undergraduate research process. *The Journal of Academic Librarianship* 22, no. 3: 201-208.

Leckie, Gloria J., and Anne Fullerton. 1999. Information literacy in science and engineering undergraduate education: Faculty attitudes and pedagogical practices. *College and Research Libraries* 60, no. 1: 9-29.

Ren, Wen-Hua. 2000. Attending to the relational aspects of the faculty citation search. *The Journal of Academic Librarianship* 26, no. 2: 119-123.

Snavely, Loanne, and Natasha Cooper. 1997. Competing agendas in higher education: Finding a place for information literacy. *Reference and User Services Quarterly* 37, no. 1: 53-62.

Stahl, Aletha D. 1997. "What I want in a librarian": One new faculty member's perspective. *Reference and User Services Quarterly* 37, no. 2: 133-135.

Stein, Linda L., and Jane M. Lamb. 1998. Not just another BI: Faculty-librarian collaboration to guide students through the research process. *Research Strategies* 16, no. 1: 29-39.

Winner, Marian C. 1998. Librarians as partners in the classroom: An increasing imperative. *Reference Services Review* 26, no. 1: 25-30.

Librarians Grading:
Giving A's, B's, C's, D's, and F's

Nicole J. Auer
Ellen M. Krupar

SUMMARY. The authors will discuss two innovative methods of increasing the teaching roles of librarians by designing and grading assignments that count towards students' final grades.

One of the authors has expanded her teaching role on campus by being involved in the development of Virginia Tech's First-Year Seminar. She participates in the design of lesson plans and serves as a facilitator for one of the fourteen sections. This includes all of the professor roles: meeting with the class once a week, working with the Student Teaching Assistant, assigning and grading assignments, holding office hours, facilitating class discussions, and dealing with course management and grading issues.

The other author is integrated within a junior-level course with at least four contacts with the students. Three training sessions include hands-on practice in the database and in-class and homework assignments. The six assignments are 15% of the final grade in the course. The author has total control of this segment of the course: design of the assignments, teach-

Nicole J. Auer is College Librarian for English, and Ellen M. Krupar is College Librarian for Business, both at Virginia Polytechnic Institute & State University (Virginia Tech).

Address correspondence to the authors at: University Libraries, P.O. Box 90001, Blacksburg, VA 24062.

[Haworth co-indexing entry note]: "Librarians Grading: Giving A's, B's, C's, D's, and F's." Auer, Nicole J., and Ellen M. Krupar. Co-published simultaneously in *The Reference Librarian* (The Haworth Information Press, an imprint of The Haworth Press, Inc.) No. 89/90, 2005, pp. 39-61; and: *Relationships Between Teaching Faculty and Teaching Librarians* (ed: Susan B. Kraat) The Haworth Information Press, an imprint of The Haworth Press, Inc., 2005, pp. 39-61. Single or multiple copies of this article are available for a fee from The Haworth Document Delivery Service [1-800-HAWORTH, 9:00 a.m. - 5:00 p.m. (EST). E-mail address: docdelivery@haworthpress.com].

http://www.haworthpress.com/web/REF
Digital Object Identifier: 10.1300/J120v43n89_04

ing of the courses, grading of the assignments, and dealing with grading issues.

The authors find that these expanded roles lead to deeper relationships with the teaching faculty and the students, due to the increased involvement. *[Article copies available for a fee from The Haworth Document Delivery Service: 1-800-HAWORTH. E-mail address: <docdelivery@ haworthpress.com> Website: <http://www.HaworthPress.com> © 2005 by The Haworth Press, Inc. All rights reserved.]*

KEYWORDS. Grading, business, marketing, library assignments, research assignments, first year experience, First-Year Seminar, course-integrated instruction, librarian-faculty collaboration

INTRODUCTION

Librarians have come a long way in the past thirty years of bibliographic instruction evolution. Hannelore Rader has provided a careful record of this evolution through her annual literature reviews published in *Library Trends*; "over 5000 publications related to library user instruction and information literacy have been published and reviewed in the past thirty years" (Rader, p. 242).[1] Today librarians are not only integrating Information Literacy into their teaching, but they are also going beyond the traditional library instruction model by teaching for-credit First-Year Seminar or Information Literacy courses, team-teaching courses in the majors, and taking leadership roles on campus to reshape the curriculum.[2]

One such article describing these new opportunities is Sarah Blakeslee's 1998 *Reference Services Review* article, where she provides a wonderfully realistic and humorous account of her experience teaching a semester-long Freshman Orientation course.[3] Elizabeth O. Hutchins and Bonnie S. Sherman discuss their collaboration with Psychology faculty that led to the revision of a biopsychology course where scholarly research was worth 40% of the grade and "the psychology professor and librarian shared the instruction and assessment of this part of the course and graded different aspects of it."[4] However, there is surprisingly little discussion of grading issues in the library literature. Patricia Woodard writes of the experience Hunter College librarians had with faculty-librarian collaboration in teaching an Honors Interdisciplinary Computer Applications course in which, "librarians graded several papers," but provides little insight into that aspect of teaching. [5] On the other hand, Deborah F. Bernnard and Trudi E. Jacobson discuss their experience on a committee that created a for-credit Information Literacy course to be included in the new General Education requirements on their campus.[6] Recognizing that teaching semester-long for-credit courses was new to most of their librarians, one of the authors scheduled several professional development workshops to increase confidence and comfort in teaching issues such as classroom management, teaching techniques, and grading (Bernnard and Jacobson, p. 139). Sadly, no details were given on these workshops. In an attempt to add to the growing literature on teaching outside of one's comfort zone, these authors hope to share their experiences with grading and all that goes with it.

OVERVIEW OF ENVIRONMENT

The instructional activities at the Virginia Tech (VT) University Libraries have been far ranging and cover all levels of learners. Grading has gradually become a larger part of our collaborations with faculty and our interactions with students. Nicole Auer's experience has been with first-year instruction and includes grading in-class worksheets and tour quizzes for English 1106, the second course in the First-Year Composition program, and serving as facilitator in VT's semester-long First-Year Seminar course called EDHL 2984 or just "The WING." Ellen Krupar's experience has been with discipline-based instruction involving the creation of a resource-based program within a junior-level marketing course and with editing article manuscripts for a leadership professional development course for Virginia law enforcement officers.

ENGLISH 1106

Within the First-Year Composition program, library research is incorporated into the second course of the sequence called English 1106 and usually taught during spring semester. Recent changes to the course curriculum have increased the library's involvement in English 1106 to include two librarian-graded components based on librarian recommendations.

Library Tour Quiz

Prior to Spring 2001, instruction for this population involved classes combining a library tour with an overview of research resources. The Director for Instruction at the University Libraries created a First-Year Services Team to develop a plan outlining the skills and instructional options for first-year students as part of the creation of a cumulating instruction program (Figure 1). To maximize the time we have with English 1106 classes, the team decided that class time would be better spent on the more complex processes such as article searching in InfoTrac and locating journal title holdings information via the online catalog. Therefore, in spring 2001, weekly tours were implemented and marketed heavily to the First-Year Composition program, including administrators, faculty, and instructors in the English department. As a result, all Graduate Teaching Assistants teaching English 1106 were required to incorporate the library tour into their syllabi. Librarians created a seven-question multiple choice quiz for the tour that was distributed and collected at the end of each tour (Figure 2). Both librarians and staff within the Instruction department graded the quizzes, which were returned to faculty who wanted attendance confirmation and who counted the quiz towards final course grades.

Trends in student scores and common errors over the past two semesters have led to changes in the wording of certain questions and to changes in the tour. Low scores on questions about locations, in conjunction with student comments from our instructional sessions, led to greater emphasis on Library of Congress call numbers. Not only did we add to our tours a handout and a demonstration of reading call numbers, but we also added a question to the tour quiz, asking students to put five call numbers in order. Keeping track of 997 quizzes during the semester has been a logistical nightmare for our Library Tours coordinator; we are currently developing a Web-based version to eliminate unclaimed or "lost" quizzes. An obvious change will be to design the quiz to fit the point value it will be worth in all sections of the course, e.g., have a ten-question quiz if it will be worth ten points.

In-Class Worksheets

In-class worksheets, originally used with the WING program during fall 2002, are another recent change to our English 1106 instruction. Using the library's First-Year Services Team's plan as a guideline, instruction has been simplified to allow for individual student work during the

FIGURE 1

First-Year Information Skills

The Virginia Tech University Libraries First-Year Services Team developed a list of information skills (stated here as learning goals) that we felt all students should acquire by the end of their first year. Other content may be added as needed for introductory courses in the majors.

- The student should be able to locate materials and service points in the library. This includes:
    - identifying locations of major service points
    - identifying locations of books and journals (bound and current)
    - understanding how the library is organized using Library of Congress call numbers.

- The student should be able to navigate the library Web site. This includes:
    - locating Addison, databases, and subject pages.

- The student should be able to find books on a research topic. This includes:
    - understanding what is and is not included in Addison [no articles from journals]
    - searching by title, author, and keyword
    - searching by keyword to identify LC subject headings for more refined searches
    - identifying parts of the citation (author, title, publisher information, and date)
    - identifying call number, location, and availability
    - searching for a periodical by title [note locations and date ranges].

- The student should be able to use a database to find articles on a research topic. This includes:
    - identifying the function of databases
    - identifying different types of databases [subject specific vs. cross-discipline]
    - using basic keyword searching techniques using a sample database like Infotrac's Expanded Academic ASAP
    - identifying parts of the citation (author, article title, journal title, volume, issue number, pages, and date).

- The student should be able to evaluate Web pages. This includes:
    - identifying evaluation criteria
    - applying strategies to gather information about Web pages
    - coming to a conclusion about the validity and reliability of Web pages.

last fifteen minutes of each instructional session. After learning about the online catalog and InfoTrac's Expanded Academic Index ASAP, students explore their own topics to identify one article and one book needed to complete the worksheet (see Appendix 1). If time permits, students then go into the collections to pull one of the items they found through online resources. Not only do students get a head start (in most cases) with their *own* research, but librarians also get a quick assessment of whether students "got" the skills covered in class.

Correcting these worksheets, approximately 1,600 during spring 2003, has been done primarily by three members of the Instruction department. While no points are currently given for this exercise across the board, librarians assign a check plus ($\sqrt{+}$), a check ($\sqrt{}$), or a check minus ($\sqrt{-}$) to the three major sections: journal article citation, journal holdings information/article location information, and book citation. Librarians

FIGURE 2. Newman Library Tour Quiz

1. Name _____Today's date _____

☐ Freshman   ☐ Sophomore   ☐ Junior   ☐ Senior   ☐ Grad   ☐ Other

2. Current newspapers and periodicals are found on what floor?

☐ 1st floor   ☐ 2nd floor   ☐ 3rd floor   ☐ 4th floor   ☐ 5th floor

3. Where would you go to get a book on reserve?

☐ 1st floor   ☐ 2nd floor   ☐ 3rd floor   ☐ 4th floor   ☐ 5th floor

4. Where would you find a 1901 issue of *The New York Times* on microfilm?

☐ 1st floor   ☐ 2nd floor   ☐ 3rd floor   ☐ 4th floor   ☐ 5th floor

5. Where would you find a *bound* volume of **The Journal of American Folklore** (call number GR1 J8)?

☐ 1st floor   ☐ 2nd floor   ☐ 3rd floor   ☐ 4th floor   ☐ 5th floor

6. Where would you go to create an account on your Hokie Passport for photocopies?

☐ Cashier's window   ☐ Circulation   ☐ Reference Desk   ☐ Inter-library Loan

7. Indicate the correct order for these call numbers by noting which should come first, second, etc.:

____HD8066 L38   ____HD8066 J38   ____HD806 L298   ____HD8066 L3224   ____HD806.6 L34

8. List two places to go for help: 1. _____2. _____

9. Did your professor require you to take a tour? ☐ YES   ☐ NO

   If yes, Course: _____ Instructor's name: _____

   Course meets (days and time): _____

verify all citations and journal holdings information and correct any discrepancies or errors. Helpful comments are included where appropriate.

Most students have done fairly well with this exercise, although the mental leap from an article citation to the journal holdings record in the online catalog continues to be the hardest part for students. As a result, we will continue to focus most of our class time with first-year students to this particular aspect of research. The spring 2003 semester has also been a valuable experience for librarians to fine-tune the process of consistently administering and correcting the in-class worksheets. Beginning in spring 2004, *all* 130 sections of English 1106 were to begin visiting the library and using this exercise as part of the course grade. This change came about because of the increased integration of information skills into the Composition curriculum.

MARKETING SKILLS 3154 COURSE

A more elaborate discipline-based instructional activity of the Virginia Tech librarians has been Ellen Krupar's involvement in the Marketing 3154 course, Marketing Skills. The focus of the course is to teach the students, most at the junior level, all of the skills that they would need out in the corporate marketing world, including marketing case studies, dining etiquette, ethics challenges and research skills. The library skills part of the course is focused on resource-based instruction, with students gaining hands-on experience with three searching systems: Factiva, LexisNexis, and RDS. The RDS session also incorporates applying searching techniques to other searching systems, with the InfoTrac and Proquest searching systems being explored briefly. The assignments make up 15% of the final grade for the course. The grades are composed of an in-class assignment and a homework assignment for each searching system, with each assignment counting for 2.5% of the final grade for the semester (see Appendixes 2 and 3 for sample assignment and grading rubrics).

The hands-on sessions are outside of the regular class meeting except for during summer session. To maximize attendance levels, ten sessions per searching system were scheduled to avoid conflicts with the typical junior-level student's schedule. The sessions were originally taught so that the three searching systems were taught in sequence: Factiva, LexisNexis and then RDS. That seemed confusing to students, who often misread the date or time of the session or attended two sessions on the same searching system. As a result, there are now three weeks of sessions, Factiva taught the first week, LexisNexis the second, and RDS the third, with the skills learned each week building upon each other. The training sessions consist of the librarian walking the students through model searches in the searching system. Students would then complete an in-class assignment with the help of the librarian and then receive a homework assignment. The librarian had established office hours both in the business school and the library to make it easier for the students to seek help on the assignments . . . which they mainly did the day before.

All sessions were taught within the business school building, which was announced in the initial meeting with the class and was on all of the sign-up sheets for the sessions. However, there was usually at least one student per semester who would mistakenly look for the session in the library. Even with ten sessions available per searching system, some students with full schedules due to university sports and work needed individual sessions, which were provided if the student could give proof of the conflicting schedule. If a student missed all ten of the sessions and had not made prior arrangements for individual sessions, acceptable excuses were: (1) death in the family, (2) sickness of the student with a doctor's note, and (3) military call-up with orders. With any of those excuses, an individual session for the student would be arranged. If none of those excuses applied, the student received a zero for the in-class assignment and was offered help with the homework assignment.

During the creation of the assignments, the ease and fairness of grading was of great concern. The Library Skills assignments needed to be at a level to justify 15% of the final grade and still be graded within a fairly short period of time. The assignments were based on the different sections of the databases and the information that could be retrieved. The in-class assignment was created to reinforce student learning during the training session and to enable the students to ask questions while they explored the searching systems. The homework assignment was designed to test students' ability to navigate and retrieve information from the searching systems. Along with directed searches, such as finding two articles on consumer preference in selection of ethnic restaurants, students were given the opportunity to search on their own topics and report on the results.

At the end of every semester, the professor and librarian discussed revisions to the assignments and different ways of administering them to the class. If a particular question seemed to be a problem for the students, it was either revised or the teaching method for that section of the class was re-examined. Because the most recent semester saw an increase in the number of students who had trouble identifying the difference between an article and a company report, differentiating between document types will be an area of focus for next semester. Another area of confusion was interpreting the article citation; the difference between volume, issue and page numbers seemed particularly difficult. Feedback was also generated by having students reply to an e-mail survey on the sessions and assignments. Also, sessions and assignments were revised each semester to incorporate any changes in the searching systems themselves, with the change from Dow Jones to Factiva as an example. Recently, the idea of giving the in-class assignments online has become attractive. A test was done with two in-house Web-based quiz programs, but they were not powerful enough and the test was turned into a survey of basic business knowledge. Due to this, the most recent set of students had only the homework assignments as graded work. Without the reinforcement of in-class assignments, grades were substantially lower. A more advanced test has been implemented using the commercial Blackboard software. The hope is to reduce the grading burden by having the software grade the in-class assignments and to accelerate how quickly the students know their grades for the in-class assignments. This will also give the students the in-class assignments back quickly enough to give them something to refer to when working on the homework assignments.

THE WING:
VIRGINIA TECH'S FIRST-YEAR SEMINAR COURSE

Virginia Tech's First-Year Seminar course, called The WING program, is a three-credit learning community course offered each fall semester. It is coordinated through the Residential Education office and offers a curriculum focused on academic and social adjustment issues such as interpersonal relationships and study skills. Faculty and staff are recruited from across campus to serve as course facilitators and are compensated through professional development money. Student Teaching Assistants, who have been through the WING program, are assigned to each of the thirteen sections of the course and help lead two weekly classes.

Librarians are involved on four levels with this program. In the broadest sense, librarians have been involved in the overall development of the program through participation on the two committees that set the syllabus and create/modify the weekly lesson plans, while the program's coordinator generally designs assignments based on the course topics. On a second level, librarians have been involved with the WING program through collaborations with the program's coordinator since 1997 to integrate research skills into the curriculum. Research has increasingly become a larger part of the course and is now a component of the final group paper/presentation related to campus issues faced by college students. During the fall 2002 semester, the library was scheduled in two places in the syllabus; both the weekly library tours and in-class instruction were included.

On a third level, librarians are involved in the WING program through their administration of the two research-related assignments. The first was the library tour quiz also used with English 1106. Students were required to take one of the weekly library tours during the first two weeks of class and received up to ten points for the library tour quiz. Although the entire library tour quiz grading process had been established the prior semester, because of the English 1106 course changes, collecting, grading, and sending the quizzes back to the appropriate facilitators proved to be a challenge. While the process was smooth in most cases, several students who claimed to have taken the library tour did not get a graded quiz back, leaving the facilitator in the awkward position of believing the student and awarding points anyway or not assigning points for the quiz. As previously mentioned, we are working to implement a Web-based quiz to eliminate these administrative problems.

Research instruction for the WING program was scheduled during week nine, and eight librarians were recruited to teach these classes. A brief orientation was held for the librarians to provide an overview of the course and the instructional session they were to teach. Fall 2002 was the first time an in-class worksheet was required and assigned twenty points towards students' final grades. Several of the recruited librarians also assisted with correcting all 150 in-class worksheets. Students generally did well on the worksheet, but their difficulty in locating the appropriate journal holdings information for their chosen article proved that in-class instruction needed to emphasize this process during English 1106 instruction in spring semester, as previously noted.

The fourth level of library participation is serving as facilitators for two of the 13 sections of this course during Fall 2002. This was new territory for our librarians and involved grading all course assignments, including weekly journals, five reflective papers, a portfolio of coursework demonstrating newly-acquired academic skills, and a research-based group presentation and related paper. There was a brief orientation for facilitators shortly before the beginning of the fall semester but grading techniques were not covered. Each facilitator was given the flexibility to grade how s/he saw fit.

Grading the writing assignments in this course was very different from grading or correcting any librarian-created activities used during instructional sessions. The time required to grade the first set of reflective papers was much greater than for subsequent papers. After delving head-first into this process, it soon became apparent that consistency and fairness were important; however, it was also remarkably easy to sort the papers from well-written to poorly-written after an initial pass over all of them. Once the papers were in rough order from best to worst, nitty-gritty details needed to be addressed before actual grading could begin, such as "How should I distribute the points?" and "What components should I weigh the heaviest?" It didn't take long before a rough grading rubric took shape (see Appendix 4). As if by providence, the Virginia Tech Center for Excellence in Undergraduate Teaching offered a workshop led by an English Instructor on how to grade/evaluate writing assignments. A useful grading rubric was distributed, discussed, and eventually guided my approach to grading the WING papers (see Appendix 5). In the end, I decided that fully completing each assignment and following its directions were paramount. Therefore, I assigned the most points (out of twenty-five per paper) to each question posed in the assignment, slightly fewer points to grammar issues (my personal pet peeve), and to each stylistic requirement (coversheet, honor system coversheet, font size, margins, etc.).

By the end of the semester, my grading system was established and seemed to work well. I could quickly modify my rubric for the current assignment and easily sort the papers by quality because I knew which elements were most important in my grading scheme. On multiple levels, our successful involvement in this program has encouraged more librarians to participate in this learning community.

INSTITUTE FOR LEADERSHIP IN CHANGING TIMES (ILCT)

Another discipline-specific program is the Institute for Leadership in Changing Times sponsored by the Virginia Police Chiefs Association and created by the Management and Professional Development Programs of the Pamplin College of Business. The goal of the program is to give mid-level law enforcement managers leadership, business and management skills that will further their career and enhance performance of their duties. As part of this, the attendees are sorted into groups and are charged with writing a manuscript to be submitted to the journal, *Virginia Police Chiefs*. As the College Librarian for Business, Ellen Krupar taught an instruction session on the process of writing research articles, including working in groups, researching a business topic, meeting deadlines for the parts of the manuscript and selecting a type of original research for them to pursue. Once a draft was written, both of these authors edited the manuscripts extensively. While no official grades were given, many revisions were required before manuscripts were submitted to the *Virginia Police Chiefs*.

In the ILCT program, the final goal was to have articles published in the *Virginia Police Chiefs*, and total freedom was given by the program administrators to achieve this goal. After consulting with Nicole Auer, as the College Librarian for English, roles were created for each group member: main author, editor, and researchers. The main author for each group was responsible, along with the group's editor, for writing the introduction, background and conclusion section of the article as well as for smoothing transitions between researcher's material. The editor within the group was responsible for helping the main author write the non-research section and for editing the document at each stage. The researchers were responsible for applying what they had learned about a business topic to their workplace or investigating how it could be applied to their work. The researchers would also be responsible for reviewing the drafts of their articles as they were submitted.

The articles did not progress totally smoothly, with some groups having members that did not participate or send in their material. Others' manuscripts required extensive editing and cutting to meet writing standards. Some groups had main authors or editors that were heavily involved with trying to catch the D.C. sniper so it is understandable that their thoughts were not focused on writing articles.

LESSONS LEARNED

Although every institution has its own unique student body, there are several common lessons we've learned from our combined experience of eight years with grading different kinds of assignments and working with different levels of students.

IT'LL TAKE LONGER THAN YOU EVER IMAGINED

Kimberley Donnelly found that for-credit courses ate up quite a bit of time, "a lot more time than any of us expected" (Donnelly, paragraph 20).[7] This echoes the experience of these authors. Even if you get work release for the addition of grading responsibilities, you will have to carve out at least half of your work week for creating and revising assignments, fielding student questions and complaints about the assignment and/or the grade, dealing with lost or incomplete assignments, and communicating with course instructors. Blakeslee so aptly summarizes this feeling when she refers to teaching as "the black hole for time" (Blakeslee, p. 76.) Before diving in, consider the amount of time required for teaching and grading any future research assignment in terms of salary dollars per hour and any compensation offered. Although teaching a for-credit course provides valuable opportunities not yet available to all librarians, such as developing long-term relationships with students, it can also turn out to be costly in terms of time lost for other projects or from the librarian's personal life.

ESTABLISH RAPPORT OR CONTROL: YOUR CHOICE

From the beginning, lay out expectations for the assignment and emphasize that you are no-nonsense. Be up front with them and they'll be up front with you. Humor is a useful tool and can help you communicate the expectations for the class in a non-confrontational way. Depending on your teaching style, you might be able to create a rapport with the students that can make the classes more interesting. One of the authors uses humor by asking questions of students related either to the library session or general business knowledge to increase their engagement in discussion and keep them aware of the need to pay attention. The point is also made to students that yawning puts them at the top of the list to answer the next question. Occasionally, this style, known to her colleagues as "picking on the students," leads to nicknames being given to the students. A student was caught playing a pinball game in class, immediately making him the person who got to answer the next three questions and earning him the nickname, "pinball wizard." Students, admittedly outgoing marketing students, did seem to appreciate being singled out, often reminding the librarian of a previously given nickname or even signing their assignments with their nicknames. However, the important thing is to establish standards of behavior within the class. In the same set of marketing skills classes, the librarian was making a joke about the number of yawns in a class and a student replied that the reason was that the class was boring. The librarian invited the student to make use of the door and reminded the student that college was not high school with ashtrays and it was his choice to remain or to leave. After a shocked silence, the student opted to stay.

SHARED EXPERIENCES LEADS TO SENSE
OF COMMUNITY WITH TEACHING FACULTY

Kimberly Donnelly said in her 2000 *Computers in Libraries* article that librarians at her institution who taught a for-credit information literacy course felt that their experience made them feel "equal with other faculty" and that they "now understand what it means to teach a course: class preparation, revising, grading and dealing with students" (Donnelly, para. 17). One of these authors experiences this community-building with faculty through participation in both the Undergraduate Honor System and in the Faculty Senate. As part of the Undergraduate Honor System, the author participates in honor panels that hear cases of suspected academic integrity violations. Initially, the students running the honor panels were hesitant to have a librarian as the faculty member representative on the honor panel. They were reassured that the librarian had created and graded assignments as well as turned students in to the honor system based on those assignments.

Within the Faculty Senate, one of the authors found that much of the networking with faculty from other departments consists of discussing class assignments and dealing with students. Often, bringing her own experience would lead to educating the faculty on the different things that the library faculty did, including grading assignments.

"IT'S ONLY FAIR IF YOU MAKE AN EXCEPTION FOR ME"

Something unexpected by these authors was how often students presumed that the grading for the library assignments would be easier than the "real" course assignments and also how often the students did not read the syllabus. Many of the students in the Marketing Skills course did not even understand that the library assignments would be graded and then expected credit just for trying. In reply to a query from a student about whether the student would get credit for writing his name on the assignment, the librarian, out of frustration, suggested that if he could not remember how to spell his name, perhaps he did not need to be in college.

A partial solution was to give an introduction to the library assignments at the beginning of the course and warn the students that these were not "blow-off" assignments. This was not always possible due to the scheduling of the class, but a notable difference was seen in the seriousness of the students when the introduction took place. However, there still was a residual expectation that a librarian would not be a hard grader. Students continued to be surprised that leaving pages of the assignments blank would result in low grades. Even telling the students that the lowest grade ever recorded in the assignments was a 3% did not seem to make sufficient impact.

Another side effect of giving assignments was dealing with the complaints and requests for grade changes. These take up a substantial amount of time, and often are spurious complaints. Unfortunately, students often did not take the Marketing Skills library assignments seriously until after they received a poor grade. Then they were quick to blame bad teaching and time pressures for incomplete or incorrect assignments. Another surprise was the number of students who dropped their requests for grade changes after being asked for rationales. When responsible for graded assignments, librarians may be played against the professor by students hoping to get their way. The Marketing Skills professor generally referred all grading questions to the librarian; however, some students did try. The professor would sometimes give in just to get the student out of his office, which would undermine the librarian and the goals of the library assignments.

Some students also wait until the last minute and then demand individual attention and instruction. For example, one of the authors had a student contact her on the third to last day of classes wanting partial credit for assignments that were three months late. Some students also feel it unnecessary to attend class and then ask for, or copy from friends, the assignments they missed. Blakeslee notes,

> It didn't take me long to realize that poor attendance was also *my* problem and a problem for the students who chose to attend class regularly. Students who missed class took away class time with questions about what they had missed and with their inability to follow or complete lab assignments due to missed lectures and unacquired skills. (Blakeslee, page 76)

Even when students are in attendance, it's amazing how much they don't listen in class. You can feel like a broken record during class, but you'll be surprised by how many times you get the same questions outside of class and how often they still get it wrong on the assignment. Often the same students that complain about the class being repetitive will get the answers wrong on the assignments. Students will often reply, "it looked easy when you did it" when complaining about their grades. This reinforces the need for actual hands-on experience in library instruction classes.

IT'S ALL IN THE DETAILS

No matter how much you plan and explain and go through the assignment's instructions, students will always ask questions you haven't anticipated about the assignment and/or their grades. Be prepared to think on your feet and stick to your guns.

It is also vital that you clearly articulate the standards of academic integrity in relation to the assignments. One of the authors ended up turning students in to the university's undergraduate honor system due to copied assignments. Turning cases in to the honor system required the librarian to provide a packet of proof to the honor system, and attend a hearing of the cases. In order to reduce the chance of this happening again, a change was made to the syllabus for the course as a whole to make it clearer that the assignments were not group work. The honor system cover sheet requiring the students to sign the honor pledge was attached to every assignment. In addition to reminding the students of the honor pledge, the honor cover sheet reduced the number of assignments that were turned in without names.

THEY DO "GET IT"–JUST LATER!

Librarian-graded assignments expose students to the resources available to them and will often incorporate more active learning opportunities and therefore encourage deeper learning. Students *do* use what they've learned when future assignments require research and will often seek out the librarian they met during those first instructional sessions for a refresher. The fact that the graded library assignments "counted" means that students will remember those assignments, the accompanying instruction, and their grades, especially if they were particularly high or low. In addition, there were many student comments about how much they learned about available resources and the various ways they used these tools in other courses.

CONCLUSION

Despite the weekly, and sometimes daily, griping about students and our grading responsibilities, these authors greatly value the learning objectives of our assignments and the opportunities we have to relate better with students and faculty. Our feeling is that the learning that takes place in the instructional sessions is cemented by the assignments providing immediate reinforcement. Until the students had to use the material on their own, students either felt that they did not need any instruction or they felt entirely intimidated by the material. The grading led to the confirming or denying of these expectations. These authors also expect grading issues to play a more prominent role in librarians' teaching responsibilities as library instruction as a whole evolves into longer and more meaningful experiences with teaching faculty and students. Assessment of skills continues to dominate in higher education, and grading will continue to contribute to this endeavor. However, the demands of grading should not be overlooked in designing library instruction classes. Provisions have to be made for the time required for designing assignments, for the grading itself, and for the resulting interactions with the students. For this type of involvement to be successful, sufficient resources need to be secured beforehand. Otherwise, it would be unfair to students and the librarian. It is hoped that readers will have gained some insight into our route to teaching ourselves about grading, something that was lacking from our library schools' curricula. Librarians should look to their colleagues, to their centers for teaching excellence, and to online writing labs for helpful guidance on grading issues. From our experiences with grading, we encourage librarians to take advantage of all opportunities available to learn about instructional design and grading techniques, since teaching competencies are becoming major components of the job and of the profession.

NOTES

1. Rader, Hannelore. (2002). "Information Literacy 1973-2002: A Selected Literature Review." *Library Trends*, 51(2), 242-261. For more information on the history of library instruction, see Salony, Mary F. (1995). "The History of Bibliographic Instruction: Changing Trends from Books to the Electronic World." *Reference Librarian*, v. 51/52, 31-51.

2. Suggested readings include Pierard, Cindy and Kathryn Graves. "The Greatest Problem with Which the Library Is Confronted: A Survey of Academic Library Outreach to the Freshman Course." In: Kelly, Maurice Caitlin and Andrea Kross (eds.) *Making the Grade: Academic Libraries and Student Success.* Chicago: Association of College & Research Libraries, 2002 and MacDonald, Mary C., Rathemacher, Andrée, and Burkhardt, Joanna M. (2000). "Challenges in Building an Incremental, Multi-Year Information Literacy Plan." *Reference Services Review*, 28(3), 240-247.

3. Blakeslee, Sarah. "Librarian in a Strange Land: Teaching a Freshman Orientation Course." *RSR*, 26(2), 1998, 73-78.

4. Hutchins, Elizabeth O. and Bonnie S. Sherman. (2001). "Information Literacy and Psychological Science: A Case Study of Collaboration." In: Dewey, Barbara I. (ed.) *Library User Education: Powerful Learning, Powerful Partnerships.* Lanham, MD: Scarecrow Press, 2001, 192.

5. Woodard, Patricia. (1996). "Librarian and Faculty Collaboration in Honors 301.88: An Interdisciplinary Computer Applications Course." *Research Strategies*, 14(3), 132-144.

6. Bernnard, Deborah F. and Trudi E. Jacobson. (2002). "The Committee that Worked: Developing an Information Literacy Course by Group Process." *Research Strategies*, 18, 133-142.

7. Donnelly, Kimberly. (2000). "Reflections on What Happens When Librarians Become Teachers." *Computers in Libraries*, 20, 46-49.

APPENDIX 1. In-Class Worksheet

Name:_____   Instructor:_____

Class time: _____   Today's date:_____

FINDING ARTICLES

<u>Instructions</u>

1. On the libraries' home page, under **Online Resources**, click on **Article Searching**.
2. Click on the appropriate letter on the left of the screen to get to the database you want to search (i.e., InfoTrac's Expanded Academic Index, MLA, etc.).
3. Scroll down until you see the database you want.
4. Click on the file name.
5. Type in the white box the search terms for your subject and execute the search.
6. From the results, please answer the following questions:

Based on your search, record the following information for an article of your choice:

Search terms:		
Number of Articles found:		
ARTICLE CITATION		
Author:		
Article title:		
Journal title:		
Volume and Issue:	Year:	Pages:

NOW SEARCH FOR YOUR JOURNAL TITLE

1. On the libraries' home page, click on **ADDISON** in the top of the black rectangle on the left of the screen.
2. Click on the **WEB** version (first choice).
3. Click on **BASIC SEARCH** (first choice).
4. Pull down the menu of choices for the **SEARCH TYPE** box and choose **TITLE**:

DOES VT OWN THIS JOURNAL?	YES	NO

| If yes, record the Call Number: |

Location for your year? (stacks, currents, etc.)	What floor will this be on?

Look at the REFERENCE LINKS on the library Web site for more citation style information

ADDISON–FINDING BOOKS

Books are great when:

- you are looking for comprehensive information on a topic.
  Note that books may be broader in scope than your specific topic, i.e., 'financial management' instead of 'credit card debt among college students.'
- you want summaries of research to support an argument.
- you want to see how your topic is discussed by researchers in other subject areas or disciplines.
- you want to find historical information.

Based on your topic, search Addison and record the following information for a book of your choice

Instructions

4. On the libraries' home page, click on **ADDISON** in the top of the black rectangle on the left of the screen.
5. Click on the **WEB** version (first choice).
6. Click on **BASIC SEARCH** (first choice).
7. Pull down the menu of choices for the **SEARCH TYPE** box and choose **KEYWORD**.
8. Enter your search term(s).

Your search terms are:	
Number of books found:	
BOOK CITATION	
Author:	
Title:	
Publisher:	Year:
Call Number:	
Location:	What floor will this be on? (if NEWMAN)
Availability:	

APPENDIX 2

Marketing Skills
Factiva
Homework Assignment

1. Screen for companies that are: in an industry and country in which you would like to work and have a P/E Ratio of between 0-50. List the first three that appear on the list as well as the industry and country.

   Industry:

   Country:

   Company:

   Company:

   Company:

2. Retrieve Dell's summary of the business description, P/E ratio for the last 12 months, annual growth rate of revenue for the last three years and three key competitors.

   Business Description:

   P/E Ratio:

   Annual Growth Rate:

   First Key Competitor:

   Second Key Competitor:

   Third Key Competitor:

3. Retrieve the comparison report for Dell against its industry. Give the name of the industry and the dividends information for both the company and industry.

   Industry Name:

   Dividends Information:

4. Retrieve the stock prices for Dell for the last three months. If you owned this stock, would you have gained or lost money? Give the date and closing price for the latest date and the oldest date.

   Latest Date and Closing Price:

   Oldest Date and Closing Price:

   Would you have gained or lost money on this stock?

5. Search for articles about branding of Dell within the journals: *BrandWeek, Infoworld Daily News* and *Advertising Age.* Give the citation (title of article, author of article, title of journal or source, volume, dates and pages) for the first article retrieved and whether the article was actually on Dell's branding. If the article was not on Dell's branding, explain why that article was retrieved (i.e., Company name was name of a person, company was mentioned within article but another company's advertising was discussed, etc.). If the article was on Dell's branding, give the main point of the article.

   Citation:

   Was article on your company's branding?

   If not, why was the article retrieved?

   If yes, what is the main point?

APPENDIX 3

Factiva

Homework

1. Industry   4 points
   Country   3 points
   Company 1   2 points
   Company 2   2 points
   Company 3   2 points

2. Business Description   4 points
   P/E Ratio   3 points
   Annual Growth Rate   3 points
   Competitor 1   2 points
   Competitor 2   2 points
   Competitor 3   2 points

3. Industry   4 points
   Dividend Rate   3 points
   Dividend Code   3 points
   Dividend Yield   3 points
   3-Year Dividend Average   3 points
   Payout Ratio   3 points
   3-Year Payout Average   3 points
   Ex-Dividend Date   3 points
   3-Year Ann. Div. Growth   3 points

4. Latest Stock Date   3 points
   Latest Close Price   3 points
   Oldest Stock Date   3 points
   Oldest Close Price   3 points
   Right Time Period   3 points
   Gained or Lost Money   3 points

5. Title of Article   3 points
   Author   3 points
   Title of Journal   3 points
   Volume   3 points
   Pages   3 points
   Date   3 points
   On Topic?   3 points
   Reason   4 points

APPENDIX 4

Paper #3 Checklist

Name: _____

Questions:

☐ Describe the earliest memory you have of an experience with a person (people) of a cultural or ethnic group different from your own.

☐ Who or what has had the most influence in the formation of your attitudes and opinions about people in different cultural groups? In what way?

☐ What influences in your experiences have led to the development of positive feelings about your own cultural heritage and background?

☐ What influences in your experiences have led to the development of negative feelings, if any, about your own cultural heritage or background?

☐ What changes, if any, would you like to make in your own attitudes or experiences in relation to people of other ethnic or cultural groups?

☐ Describe any experiences in your own life when you feel you were discriminated against for any reason, not necessarily because of your culture.

_____

OVERALL:

☐ flow of paper–easy to read (not wordy, awkward, or choppy)

☐ all questions answered (from the full description of the assignment) in an organized essay format (not simply listed)

☐ grammar (esp. comma issues)

☐ all directions followed–paper format and standard coversheet

Comments:

APPENDIX 5

Writing Assessment Checklist				
Criteria	Excellent	Fair	Poor	Comments
Conception–				
Has the writer told you something you didn't already know? Something that wasn't obvious?				
What is the writer's purpose? Does he/she accomplish his/her purpose?				
Is the work appropriate for the audience?				
Are alternative or opposing views considered?				
If the writer has presented something you already knew, did he/she at least get you thinking about it in a different way?				
Can the reader follow the overall structure?				
Strategy–				
Is the supporting material persuasive?				
Are ideas well-developed?				
Is unnecessary repetition of ideas avoided?				
Do the major ideas receive enough attention?				
Are ideas expressed clearly?				
Is each paragraph unified, developed, organized, and coherent?				
Are paragraphs the right length for reading (not too long or too short)?				
Style–				
Is the word choice appropriate for the audience?				
Are transitions used?				
Are sentences varied?				
Is vocabulary varied?				
Is interesting language used (e.g., metaphors, language that appeals to the senses, etc.)?				
Are strong verbs (e.g., not "to be" verbs) and vivid nouns used? Is wordiness avoided?				
Grammar and Mechanics–				
Are punctuation and spelling correct?				
Are sentences grammatically correct?				
Three specific changes for this work or three particular strengths of this paper are: 1. 2. 3.				

Reproduced by permission from Lisa Norris, Department of English, Virginia Tech.

Can't Get No Respect:
Helping Faculty to Understand
the Educational Power
of Information Literacy

William B. Badke

SUMMARY. While there is much discussion today about information literacy, proper implementation of it within university campuses is still a struggle, often due to the fact that librarians and teaching faculty have different "cultures" that create different priorities. Librarians focus more on process and faculty more on content, though the two are not mutually exclusive. Past attempts by librarians to collaborate with faculty to produce information literate students have had limited success. A bolder plan–to imbed information literacy credit courses within existing departments–shows promise to avoid cultural conflict while creating a proper climate for collaboration. *[Article copies available for a fee from The Haworth Document Delivery Service: 1-800-HAWORTH. E-mail address: <docdelivery@haworthpress.com> Website: <http://www.HaworthPress.com> © 2005 by The Haworth Press, Inc. All rights reserved.]*

William B. Badke is Associate Librarian, Trinity Western University, for Associated Canadian Theological Schools and Information Literacy, 7600 Glover Road, Langley, BC, Canada V2Y 1Y1 (E-mail: badke@twu.ca).

[Haworth co-indexing entry note]: "Can't Get No Respect: Helping Faculty to Understand the Educational Power of Information Literacy." Badke, William B. Co-published simultaneously in *The Reference Librarian* (The Haworth Information Press, an imprint of The Haworth Press, Inc.) No. 89/90, 2005, pp. 63-80; and: *Relationships Between Teaching Faculty and Teaching Librarians* (ed: Susan B. Kraat) The Haworth Information Press, an imprint of The Haworth Press, Inc., 2005, pp. 63-80. Single or multiple copies of this article are available for a fee from The Haworth Document Delivery Service [1-800-HAWORTH, 9:00 a.m. - 5:00 p.m. (EST). E-mail address: docdelivery@haworthpress.com].

KEYWORDS. Information literacy, faculty culture, collaboration, librarians, professional respect, accreditation, ACRL, information professionals, credit courses

INTRODUCTION

Information literacy appears to be on a roll. With new sets of standards and best practices released by ACRL,[1] and with accrediting bodies looking seriously at incorporating those standards into their criteria,[2] it seems that the longsuffering voices in the wilderness who have fought against great odds to introduce info lit into the curriculum have been rewarded. In fact, studies in the past ten years have shown that most faculty rate library research instruction as very important.[3]

Yet the struggle continues, with librarians still finding minimal support–in finance, personnel, and teaching venues–for credible information literacy programs. We continue to do one-shot generic and subject-specific sessions, as well as offering point-of-need guidance at the reference desk, recognizing that such "training" does not even begin to make a student literate within the world of information. Christine Bruce, commenting on information literacy discourse, writes: "It has been evident that little of the literature is appearing in mainstream higher education journals or discipline-based journals, suggesting that the transformation of the information literacy agenda from a library-centered issue to a mainstream educational issue is only beginning."[4]

The problem, many academic librarians insist, is obstreperous faculty. Faculty are perceived as giving lip service to the need for a student body properly schooled in research skills, offering only limited opportunity for students in their courses to develop those skills, and standing by the long-held false assumption that students develop their abilities simply by being sent to the library to use its resources. In fact, even when faculty do give librarians an hour of their teaching time, they often do not attend class themselves, despite the fact that many a faculty member is less aware of the new technologies than the average student.[5]

Academic librarians are the Rodney Dangerfields of the academic world–they can't get no respect. I recently remarked on this fact to a police officer friend of mine, pointing out that he and I were alike when it came to lack of respect given our vocations. He smiled and said, "No, we're not alike. I have a gun and pepper spray." That leaves librarians in a category to themselves. A seemingly endless line of surveys have shown consistently that faculty members do not see librarians as true faculty, often have little understanding of the skills of librarians and cannot even distinguish between professionals and non-professionals in the libraries of their own institutions.[6]

Librarians, for their part, regularly report that faculty do not know the library's resources, and send students to do research on ambiguous assignments requiring the use of materials that the library does not have.[7] Faculty are regarded as emperors to themselves, eccentric and lacking understanding of most anything outside of their narrow circles of interest. The extent of librarian frustration with faculty is often unspoken, but when words are uttered, they are telling, as in a recently overheard comment from an academic librarian to about 50 of her peers: "Librarians have to be professionals. Faculty don't." Her words were greeted by all with understanding and approval.

We thus exist in a context that is typified, to cite a Canadian expression, by "two solitudes." Faculty do not respect the roles of librarians, and librarians view faculty as arrogantly ignorant of the functioning of the library, its personnel and its tools. Such a context does not bode at all well for information literacy, since it is generally the librarians who first see the need for improving student information skills but the faculty and administration who hold the keys to implementing effective training.

How, then, can librarians, lacking respect, move faculty to understand the educational power of the sort of information literacy profound enough actually to take us beyond the inadequate abilities we now see in our students year after year?

THE ROLE OF FACULTY CULTURE

The value of Larry Hardesty's 1995 study of faculty culture to this issue can scarcely be over-estimated. Hardesty demonstrated that at the heart of librarian-faculty misunderstanding is the interplay of two distinct cultures. Whereas librarians typify a "managerial culture" of goals, collegiality and a concern for the broader educational needs of the student, faculty culture emphasizes "research, content and specialization," with a "de-emphasis on teaching, process and undergraduates."[8] A supreme value among faculty is professional autonomy, whose corollary is academic freedom. Faculty, as well, according to Hardesty, typically face a chronic shortage of time to fulfill their tasks and are resistant to change.[9] Librarians, seeking to meet broad student informational needs and develop skills that go beyond the bounds of any particular subject discipline, are thus viewed by faculty as intruders. Hardesty writes:

In other words, faculty members who hold on to the values of faculty culture (a feeling of lack of time; emphasis on content, professional autonomy and academic freedom; de-emphasis on the applied and the process of learning; and resistance to change) are not interested in "bright ideas" from librarians about bibliographic instruction.[10]

Baker pointed out what may well be a related complication of faculty culture–the fact that faculty in discipline-related focus groups that were looking at goals for information literacy assignments tended not to see the issue in terms of broader skills for lifelong learning and the marketplace, but framed "the student library assignment decision around narrower and more directly impactive pedagogical and educational questions, such as familiarity with the literature in a specific discipline."[11] That is, faculty thought in terms of content, and specifically content within their own disciplines, rather than in terms of process and skill development that could be transferable to a wider range of subjects.

Leckie and Fullerton used the language of pedagogical discourse to explain the distinctiveness of faculty and librarian perceptions of their roles. Their conclusion was that, "Faculty are participating in discourses that serve to protect their disciplines, preserve their own disciplinary expertise and academic freedom, and uphold self-motivated, individualistic learning. Librarians are employing the pedagogical discourses related to meeting user needs, teaching important generic skills and providing efficient service."[12] They further pointed out that faculty pedagogy seeks to maintain control of the classroom, thus making it difficult for librarians to encroach into faculty held territory.[13]

Kempcke, publishing in 2002, argued that things may have changed since Hardesty. Many institutions are re-evaluating core curriculum, and the recent ACRL "Competency Standards for Higher Education,"[14] have put pressure on academia to take information literacy seriously. He writes: "No longer are we in business just to support teaching. In a sense, the tables have been turned. Undergraduate teaching needs to support the library and its instructional mission of IL. The library is not auxiliary to campus programs; it is one of them."[15] These words may well ring true in the future, but there appears to be little evidence in recent literature of movement from the entrenchment in faculty culture that Hardesty described.

Is faculty culture an obstacle to making student bodies information literate? Faculty would certainly deny any such accusation, arguing that their work of teaching the content and critical thinking skills inherent to their disciplines is information literacy at its best. Information literacy, however, as defined by ACRL and many other groups is anchored not just in content with a little critical thinking thrown in, but in process. Librarians, who generally focus more on process, find themselves hard pressed to convince faculty that knowledge of content (and even ability to think critically within content) is insufficient to make most people truly information literate.

Discipline-specific content skills, even when they come with critical thinking, are only a beginning when it comes to information literacy. Somehow the student must gain transferable strategic ability. To use an analogy, we might train a person how to steer a car, how to use the brakes, and so on, but we have not taught a person how to drive a car until these knowledge subsets are synthesized. Information literacy requires the ability to strategize research and information use regardless of what content may be encountered.

COLLABORATION AS A MOTHERHOOD ISSUE

How does any institution of higher learning achieve the goals of information literacy? The answer that always first comes to mind is "collaboration"–librarians, teaching faculty, and administrators working together for one glorious common goal. The introduction to the ACRL Standards document, for example, asserts: "Incorporating information literacy across curricula, in all programs and services, and throughout the administrative life of the university, requires the collaborative efforts of faculty, librarians, and administrators."[16]

Yet we have just seen that the priorities of librarians and teaching faculty are different, so much so that faculty members commonly resist the efforts of librarians to inject info lit into the classroom. True, collaboration does accomplish its purposes in some circumstances. Banks, Carder and Pracht have reported increased collegiality that resulted from luncheon electronic resource training sessions for faculty.[17] Mestre has offered 29 "Ways to Begin a Collaboration,"[18] and Holtze has suggested "100 Ways to Reach your Faculty."[19] Most librarians have sympathetic faculty who support their IL efforts.

But all of this points out the essence of the problem. If collaboration were happening on a broad basis, why would we need faculty luncheons, or 29 ways to begin a collaboration, or 100 ways to reach your faculty? The fact is, and the vast literature confirms it, effective collaboration simply is not the norm.

But we keep trying. Leckie and Fullerton, after chronicling the gulf between librarian and teaching faculty pedagogical priorities, assert that "librarians have an important role to play by supporting faculty in developing and broadening their own information literacy, and by assisting faculty who then feel comfortable incorporating information literacy into their teaching."[20] It appears that optimism reigns eternal, despite the clear evidence that the gulf continues intact. Are there grounds for hope that we can bridge the gap or bypass it in some way so that the goals of information literacy may be achieved?

Several paths to collaboration have been navigated. All are precarious.

LIBRARIAN AS FRIENDSHIP EVANGELIST

Having grown up in an Evangelical Christian environment, I am well aware of a now waning brand of evangelism in which the earnest Christian befriended a likely prospect with the intent to woo that person, then make a pitch that would lead to a conversion. If the prospect was resistant, a new "friend" would be sought and the old one dropped. Such an approach, not typical to modern Evangelicals, most of whom find it repugnant, reeks of hypocrisy or at least manipulation.

For any friendship evangelist, whether seeking new members for the Kingdom or an opportunity to win a faculty member to the need for information literacy training in the classroom, the goal is to make converts of those who would normally resist other types of advances. The evangelist plies them with coffee, spends time with them, flatters them, and so on. Why, one could probably think of 100 ways to reach a prospect.[21] If you believe this is a caricature of many librarian approaches to faculty, ask yourself this: Would we be going to all this effort to win faculty if our ultimate purpose were not to convince them that they need to get on board with information literacy?

The profound disadvantage of wheedling our way into the good graces of faculty in order to make a pitch about information literacy is that we come at it from a position of weakness. We become dependent on the good will of faculty, who do not have to listen to us or cut us any favors.

Winning favor from a position of weakness can lead to small victories, even the occasional big one, but you have no guarantee that your carefully prepared prospect won't turn around and bite you or simply not deliver on whatever assurances you were able to attain. Even when we do win the occasional faculty member as a supporter of our cause, it is only one faculty member among many.

LIBRARIAN AS TACTICIAN

Ken Kempcke argues that subservience is both counterproductive and a denial of our real power. He writes: "We cannot be relegated to second-rate partners in the educational process. We need bravery, not humility. Strength in our alliances. Power over our organizational environment. Not just participation, but command in campus leadership."[22]

As his handbook, Kempcke uses Sun Tsu's *The Art of War*, not as a guide to fighting battles with the academy but as a source for developing strategies that will make tactical gains. Librarians, he affirms, are now in the driver's seat because the ACRL standards on information literacy are leading to curricular reform on university campuses. As information experts, we must seize opportunities that come our way, without any sense that we are inferiors in the academy.

Rather than urging us to win favor from a position of weakness, Kemcke calls on librarians to be tacticians:

> My advice is to find a niche, to infiltrate a soft spot in the battlement—one that provides the best area to devote resources and is the most likely theatre for success. Whatever post you station, communicate its importance and defend it aggressively. Identify the right leaders to follow or befriend. Target those in your way.[23]

Heady language indeed. While still using strategies to win a hearing, Kemcke comes at it from a position of strength. After all the years of being Rodney Dangerfield, is it possible that the tide has turned? Kemcke is confident it has. He writes: "At a time when other faculty are demoralized by what their students turn in as 'research,' we remain at a higher stratum, ready and willing to sweep down with comprehensive and awe-inspiring assistance. We are formidable and skilled warriors against the forces of ignorance."[24]

But Kemcke is over-optimistic. The reality is that the tide may be turning slowly, but there is little evidence that we are about to make gains where it truly counts—in courses, personnel and funding to do the task of information literacy as it should be done. There are no large movements to implement anything like comprehensive programs we require to reach all of our students. The accrediting bodies may be rumbling in the distance about the need for information literacy in the curriculum, but the continuing experience of most academic librarians is that information literacy is only a small blip on the radar of most professors and their academic administrators. Faculty culture remains a tough nut to crack.

Kempcke's notion of a tactical approach to collaboration has some highly attractive features, but it can just as easily backfire if it turns out that we lack the clout to complete our mission. If we do not have the newly found respect he envisions, we are likely to be swatted down like bothersome flies. He is clearly aware of the problem as he stresses: "Our attacks should be designed to enlighten our colleagues as to the importance of IL in a student's life. Our goal should be to enable, not manipulate."[25] Still, no tactics will be well received if our status as librarians has not changed dramatically, as he so confidently asserts.

SHOW THEM WHAT WE CAN DO

Librarians now have an unlikely ally–the increasingly complex information systems that hold the key to most of the storehouse of the world's knowledge. Leora Baron writes: "The challenges facing today's information seeker do not even resemble the challenges of only a few years ago. The new information landscape requires competence and skills not only to locate or access information, but to make informed, discriminating choices."[26]

Since librarians are information specialists, aware of the latest nuances of the newest databases, we have a large door open to impress faculty with our expertise. The amount of opportunity today for librarians to offer support and information literacy upgrading to faculty is phenomenal. Faculty are gradually beginning to understand that their students are often more database savvy than they are. Even more significantly, faculty are recognizing that the very tools that are their stock in trade–journals, library catalogs and indexes–have not only gone electronic but have become so complex that their own research could well be hampered by their lack of knowledge of the finer details of new information systems.

Librarians to the rescue. We have the means, if we are careful at it, to astound faculty with our understanding of these systems and thus impress upon them the need to make information literacy a priority for their students. Owusu-Ansah writes:

> The environment created by these changes in the quantity of information and the resources for accessing them present a new challenge for the academic library. It represents the backdrop against which the academic library's contribution, redefined by necessity, should be demonstrated . . . To do less would be to short-change contemporary civilization.[27]

Beyond helping faculty learn how to navigate the complexities of new information tools, we are in a position to put ourselves forward as information experts who can help them with many aspects of their research. This may smack of a tactical maneuver but actually represents a genuine contribution from a position of strength, a contribution that no one but an information professional can make. If the eyes of faculty are opened to what we can do for them, we have a much better chance of convincing them that their students need to benefit from our expertise as well. We are, after all, affirming the very thing that faculty most value–their ability to serve their own disciplines well.

Yet this approach, as promising as it may appear, still depends on faculty making the second step to take what they've seen in us and translate that into a plan to enable us to reach their students. This is rarely taken unless we pursue our contacts vigorously and continue to market our opportunities with the same vigor year after year.

IS THERE HOPE?

All of the approaches we have cited–lobbying from weakness, confidently wielding tactics, or showing them what we can do–carry with them the reality that the task of bringing real information literacy to campus is a thing of much work and small victories. The weak can be stepped on or ignored, the tactician can be shown to lack the power to have influence. Even showing faculty what we can do demands that they, in turn, make the jump to allowing us access to their students. Our educational setting works against us. We are locked within an environment in which discipline-specific instruction is the norm, professors cling to their turf, and the powers that be will release neither personnel, funding, nor curriculum space to enable a wider information literacy enterprise to take root.

We could wait for accrediting bodies to determine what is needed and put teeth into demands that we produce information literate students, but a look at recent changes in accreditation standards is less than encouraging. Most use the term "information literacy," but describe its implementation with vague criteria such as, "evidence of information literacy incorporated into the curriculum" (MSACS), "ensure that the use of the library and information resources is integrated into the learning process" (NASC), and so on.[28] Such statements are already being met minimally in most institutions, or can be argued to have been met, though they do not amount to real information literacy. It is thus doubtful that we can count on Big Brother to bring in a big stick, at least not in the short term.

Unless academic librarians put an innovative step forward, it appears that we are doomed to repeat the past decades, ever trying to convince faculty that genuine information literacy is a crucial educational value, ever being looked on ourselves as people who should stay off the protective lawns of academia. We need a breakthrough, something bolder and more convincing than all the weedling, strategizing and self-promotion we have been doing.

A WAY FORWARD

To find a new path, we must consider the resources we have to offer, the nature of the task to be done, and the means to make it happen. Obviously, going down old paths, even deviously tactical ones, is not going to move us a substantial distance ahead. Fresh thinking is needed.

First let us consider our personal resources. The average reference librarian, beyond providing access to the physical collections and technological tools, has an expertise that must not be discounted. Mary Biggs has described it well:

> We are information professionals, which is to say, society authorities on the generation, nature, promotion and use of recorded information and ideas–and society's preeminent defenders of their integrity and right to be exposed. These are remarkable charges and carry with them the responsibility to teach.[29]

We may or may not be subject specialists as are historians or chemists, but we are process specialists who have both the philosophical foundations and the skills to acquire, evaluate and put to use information coming from most any discipline. Who else but a reference librarian could, in a single shift on the desk, help a student identify larvae drawings taken from life in a nearby pond, locate a photograph on the Internet with only minimal clues as to its content, help a professor locate missing details in a muddled citation, find a copy of the legal judgment against Galileo, and come up with twenty years of detailed statistics on pig populations in Canada region by region?

This gift of ours is not just a skill. It is a trained art that involves understanding of how information operates, ability to use the tools to find it almost magically, and critical thinking to evaluate it by methods that have become instinctive. We have a nose for information, like the nose of a bloodhound.

All of this begs the question of whether we are, or are not, subject specialists. Perhaps we should be seen as masters of a subject area that is *information itself*. Perhaps information, its discovery and proper use, should be viewed as its own subject.

What is our task in the enterprise of information literacy? At one time the answer seemed easy–Our task is to help our students learn how to use a library so they can write their research papers. Now, with so many information sources available even in the middle of the desert to a patron with a computer and an Internet link, the answer is less clear.

If we put the question instead into the context of more ultimate goals, it takes on a new face. We could continue to limit our vista to helping students to research their papers, but the new accessibility of information resources, of which the physical library is only a part, opens the door for us to look beyond what the student needs for the here and now, and ask a deeper question: *What do our students need in order to navigate the new world of information for the rest of their lives?* Perhaps one of the main reasons why we have so long battled with faculty over the need for students to know how to do research is that our goals were too small. We've been insisting that students need better research skills so that they can write better papers, and faculty have been retorting that the existing research papers are not all that bad, so students must be learning the skills on their own.

Ensuring that students have the tools for lifelong learning is a much bigger prospect, one which would appear to be a given but which usually finds little place in the curriculum. Surely, if it is true that we cannot teach students all they need for the rest of their lives, sending them out as graduates who can meet the basic ACRL standards for information literacy would appear to be a basic requirement for a good education.

If this is the objective, then the means to achieve it takes focus. Clearly one-shot and point-of-need training, while helpful in themselves, cannot hope to make a lifelong skilled researcher who can cross subject disciplines in the intelligent quest for the right information. Subject specialized instruction does not generally create skills that are transferable to other realms of study.

How, then, can true information literacy instruction be accomplished without being too subject specific or too generic, without invading faculty space but at the same time not being too peripheral?

Perhaps the most promising and relatively new approach is *to embed credit-bearing information literacy courses within departments.* The intention is to give such courses homes within subject disciplines, where they can be informed by the content that students with majors require while at the same time having the flexibility to include a broader philosophy of information as well as the skills to do informational research beyond a single subject. Such courses can begin as electives, gain popularity, and then move toward becoming part of the core, either because departmental faculty see the light or because accrediting bodies eventually demand it.

Several scholars have argued that information literacy at a high level needs to be the right of every student, regardless of what inroads (or lack of them) librarians have made into resistant faculty culture. Owusu-Ansah writing on the need to provide a structure for the development of institution-wide information literacy asks: "Why not then have independent courses for the provision of such a structure? What should be done with the students in courses with uncooperative faculty? Are they not to receive the crucial skills that library instruction can provide?"[30]

To create a broadly based generic information literacy curriculum that is designated with a LIBR or UNIV tag is to take it out of the hands of faculty who, despite their autonomous culture, need and likely want to take some ownership of a program of information literacy in the curriculum. Students learning information skills do, after all, require content. True, there are several large generic programs that seem to be succeeding, but careful scrutiny would show that this is only because of very strong support from senior academic administration and a great deal of zealous effort from the librarians who teach them.

If we believe that information literacy is best done when content is a factor, then the most relevant contexts for credit courses are surely the departments in which students take their majors. Such departments, to be sure, are part of the turf of the faculty, but they are not the sort of central all-sacred turf that is found in the classroom. The distinction might be illustrated by the difference between my own backyard and the neighborhood park down the block. I may tolerate some strangers in the park, as long as they behave themselves, but I don't want them jumping my fence and helping themselves to my barbecue or swimming pool.

A strategy at my own institution may illustrate how this embedding a credit information literacy course within a department can be accomplished. Our head librarian and I had long wanted to develop a three-credit information literacy course on our campus. We decided this was going to happen only if we offered the course to the institution for "free" (meaning that the library would absorb the cost of its donated librarian time within its existing budget) and if we could find a department head who could be made an enthusiastic supporter. We chose the Communications Department, both because its head had already seen the value of information literacy, and because Communications, by its very definition, deals directly with many varieties of information and information systems.

The department head greeted the idea of a new elective course within his department with enthusiasm. Other faculty in the department raised no objections and saw some potential value in such a course. Armed with a strong proposal and syllabus, we presented it to our Undergraduate Academic Committee. There was a surprisingly positive response to the idea of using credit hours to teach students how to "do research," but there were also some detractors among well-respected faculty who raised a legitimate objection. "This is a university," they argued. "We don't need yet another skills course, regardless of how fine an idea it is that our students learn how to do research."

We agreed with them. True, there is a skills element in information literacy, just as there is in many courses, but there is also a philosophy that emerges from points 3 and 5 of the ACRL standards: "The information literate student evaluates information and its sources critically and incorporates selected information into his or her knowledge base and value system"; and, "The information literate student understands many of the economic, legal, and social issues surrounding the use of information and accesses and uses information ethically and legally."[31] Bound up in those statements alone is enough "theory of" and "philosophy of" to satisfy most academics.

The Committee approved the course. It has now been taught twice, with a high level of popularity and increasing student numbers. After the first run-through it was listed as an elective in every stream within the Communications Department program. While still not within the core of the program, at least it has a place.[32] True, the library has had to donate my time, and we lack the resources at this point to expand the advance of such courses into academia, but it is a good beginning on which we can build.

A number of objections will be raised to embedding information literacy courses within departments. First, most university curricula are full, and introducing a new course is a hard sell. This is a given, but it is also a given that curricula do change over time, especially when they receive impetus from enthusiastic supporters or the demands of accreditation.

A second, and more difficult, challenge comes from that fact that there is simply not the resource base in most institutions to launch such an initiative. How many librarians will it take to move from teaching one elective course in one department to offering many elective courses in many departments to including these courses in the core curriculum of departments so that multiple sections are needed for each course? The answer is quite simply, "A lot of librarians, most of whom are currently not available."

But this is exactly the heart of the issue—we are looking at a new paradigm for the electronic information age. Many studies have shown that both the gate counts and reference interviews in academic libraries are diminishing. Students can now retrieve much of their research information without ever darkening our doors. Could it be that we are on the brink of a new paradigm for reference librarians, in which the reference desk as a location has diminishing importance and librarians are no longer defined by location but by their ability to facilitate proper use of information whatever its source and wherever the location of the patron? If we are, indeed, the information professionals on campus, then the transition from helping a student solve a point-of-need research problem at the reference desk to teaching a class full of students the rudiments of information literacy is not as large a shift as we might think.

Still, the prospect of funding and staffing what is, essentially, its own cross-departmental department, creates daunting challenges. We will definitely need more staff, and the costs will be high. But new initiatives in higher education are driven by the needs that demand them. Do we want information literate students? Yes. Have current efforts through one-shot sessions and sporadic intrusions into faculty territory succeeded in creating information literate students? No. Thus, if the job is not being done, and accrediting bodies (slowly to be sure) will at some point put teeth into demands for information literacy training, something will eventually give. At that point, personnel must be put in place and money must be available.

We need to remember that the strategy proposed will be incremental. You start with one or two elective courses, each in its own department, get support to increase the number of such courses, then look at the possibility of making them part of departmental cores. Such process will take several years. No initiative is projected to succeed overnight, thus we have time to develop our infrastructure.

Third, the implication that librarians should take the primary role in developing and teaching such courses may be seen as ignoring the necessary subject orientation of departments. Perhaps faculty could be co-opted either to teach these courses or to team teach them with librarians. This suggestion carries with it two assumptions: first, that librarians do not have subject knowledge and second, that information literacy training needs the input of faculty to be done properly.

Nothing in our proposal precludes the possibility of team teaching, though there must be one bedrock assumption–When it comes to the philosophy and skills of information literacy, librarians trump faculty. Teaching faculty within a department should certainly be involved in planning info lit courses and may well team teach within them. But librarians, many of whom have at least masters level knowledge of specific disciplines, must take the leadership role, because our purpose is to foster information literacy, not just to promote the subject needs of the discipline. Such courses would use examples and emphases related to the disciplines in which they were embedded, but their primary goal would be to teach students how information works, how research should be strategized, and how the resulting information should be handled. Unless there is a strong emphasis on transferability of skills and knowledge to other disciplines, we have not moved beyond the subject-specific classroom intrusion approach.

CONCLUSION

We began our discussion by going over the much-trodden ground of librarian-faculty collaboration encouraged in order to impress faculty with the value of information literacy training. Though collaboration appears to be foundational to making such training operational, the barriers of faculty culture continue to make info lit an unnecessary intrusion onto faculty turf. Clearly, after decades of trying to put information literacy into the mainstream of our institutions, we have seen more failures than successes.

How, then, do we impress faculty, and academic administration, with the need for extensive training of students that will represent more than lip service to the emerging standards of information literacy? The answer is not to continue invading faculty turf, but, through a combination of showing them what we have to offer and injecting credit-bearing courses into departments, to demonstrate that information skills can be taught at a much higher level, resulting in benefits to faculty members' own disciplines.

Rather than threatening faculty autonomy or carrying out our own generic programs at the fringes of academia, the real path forward is found in strategy to place information literacy within departments where they can foster departmental goals. Faculty can have input and in turn can be impressed with what we have to offer as they see such courses unfold. They are allowed to keep all of the turf that means the most to them, while at the same time seeing their students improve in their understanding of information needs and abilities within their primary disciplines.

True, it will take time. We may have to develop courses one at a time as resources come available, moving them gradually from elective to core status as department faculty and administrators see their value. This will demand new resources that will come only as we prove the worth of such training, and both accrediting bodies and academic administrators mandate this approach.

A side benefit addresses the problem of respect: If, indeed, librarians become colleagues in the teaching enterprise, then they will be faculty colleagues indeed. Some librarians may resist such a notion, stressing that they are already professionals deserving of respect, but the fact is that the world is changing. Our patrons are not coming as often to us, but we have a new opportunity to go to them. In the process, the perception of our role may well change dramatically, and academia will learn what we have long known about ourselves–that we are the true information professionals on campus.[33] Perhaps one day the word "librarian" will be spoken with awe.

NOTES

1. Available: http://www.ala.org/acrl/ilcomstan.html and http://www.earlham.edu/~libr/Plan.htm.

2. See http://www.ala.org/acrl/il/accreditation.html.

3. See, for example, Anita Canon, "Faculty Survey on Library Research Instruction," *RQ* 33, no. 4 (Summer 1994): 527-528; Gloria J. Lecki and Anne Fullerton, "Information Literacy in Science and Engineering Undergraduate Education: Faculty Attitudes and Pedagogical Practices," *College and Research Libraries* 60, no. 1 (1999): 23.

4. Christine Bruce, "Faculty-Librarian Partnerships in Australian Higher Education: Critical Dimensions," *Reference Services Review* 29, no. 2 (2001): 113.

5. Leckie and Fullerton, "Information Literacy," 23, reported a non-attendance rate of 44%. This type of rate is confirmed by several other studies.

6. See the historical analysis and survey results of Robert I. Ivey, "Teaching Faculty Perceptions of Academic Librarians at Memphis State University," *College and Research Libraries* 55, no. 1 (January 1994): 69-82. We resist, however, giving in to fellow librarian Mark Plaiss's depressing assertion that librarians, because they give information away and lack an academic philosophy for their role, are not academics, nor professionals, but should see themselves on the level of trade school graduates. Mark Plaiss, "Wheat-Paste Librarians and the Jesse Shera Band," *American Libraries* 27, no. 3 (March 1996): 29-30.

7. An extensive survey of academic librarians done in 2001 revealed that "eighty-six percent . . . believe faculty are not adequately equipped to use libraries today; 93% believe faculty are not prepared to help students use libraries today." *The Role of Librarians in a Digital Age: Preliminary Findings.* Jones e-global library. Accessed: http://www.e-globallibrary.com [13 February 2003].

8. Larry Hardesty, "Faculty Culture and Bibliographic Instruction: An Exploratory Analysis," *Library Trends* 44, no. 2 (Fall 1995): 348-351.

9. Ibid., 351-354.

10. Ibid., 356.

11. Robert K. Baker, "Faculty Perceptions Towards Student Library Use in a Large Urban Community College," *Journal of Academic Librarianship* 23, no. 3 (May 1997): 179.

12. Gloria Leckie and Anne Fullerton, "The Roles of Academic Librarians in Fostering a Pedagogy for Information Literacy." 9th ACRL Conference, Detroit, Michigan, April 8-11, 1999. Accessed: http://www.ala.org/acrl/leckie.pdf [March 25, 2003].

13. Ibid.

14. http://www.ala.org/acrl/ilcomstan.html.

15. Ken Kempcke, "The Art of War for Librarians: Academic Culture, Curriculum Reform, and Wisdom from Sun Tzu," *portal: Libraries and the Academy* 2, no. 4 (2002): 529-551.

16. Association of College and Research Libraries "Information Literacy Competency Standards for Higher Education." Available: http://www.ala.org/acrl/ilintro.html.

17. Julie Banks, Linda Carter, and Carl Pracht, "Library Luncheon and Update: Teaching Faculty about New Technology," *Journal of Academic Librarianship* 22, no. 2 (March 1996): 128-130.

18. Lori Mestre, "Collaborating with Faculty: Ideas and Selected Bibliography." Accessed: http://www.library.umass.edu/instruction/faculty/collabideas.html [March 25, 2002].

19. Terri L. Holtze, "100 Ways to Reach your Faculty," *Different Voices, Common Quest: Adult Literacy and Outreach in Libraries*: An OLOS Preconference at the American Library Association Annual Meeting Atlanta, Georgia, June 13-14, 2002. Accessed: http://www.ala.org/olos/voices/reach_faculty.pdf [March 26, 2003].

20. Leckie and Fullerton, "Roles of Academic Librarians," 8.

21. Holtze, "100 Ways."

22. Kempcke, "The Art of War," 47.

23. Ibid., 545; similar sentiments are voiced by Andrea Glover in Katherin B. Chiste, Andrea Glover, and Glenna Westwood, "Infiltration and Entrenchment: Capturing and Securing Information Literacy Territory in Academe." *Journal of Academic Librarianship* 26, no. 3 (May 2000): 206-208.

24. Ibid., 541.

25. Ibid., 538.

26. Leora Baron, "Information-Driven Teaching and Learning," *Advocate Online: Thriving in Academe*. August 2001. Accessed: http://www.nea.org/he/advo01/advo0108/feature.html [March 22, 2003].

27. Edward K. Owusu-Ansah, "The Academic Library in the Enterprise of Colleges and Universities: Toward a New Paradigm." *Journal of Academic Librarianship* 27, no. 4 (July 2001): 284.

28. For a description of the latest accrediting standards related to information literacy, see ACRL Information Literacy, "Accreditation." Accessed: http://www.ala.org/acrl/il/accreditation.html [March 24, 2003].

29. Mary Biggs, "Librarians as Educators: Assessing our Self-Image." *Public and Access Services Quarterly* 1, no. 1 (1995): 49.

30. Owusu-Ansah, 290. See also, Kempcke, 547.

31. Accessed: http://www.ala.org/acrl/ilstandardlo.html [March 25, 2003].

32. This concept is not new. I have suggested it in my article, "All We Need Is a Fast Horse: Riding Info Lit into the Academy," in *Musings, Meanderings, and Monsters, Too: Essays on Academic Librarianship*, ed. Martin Raish (Lanham, MD: Scarecrow Press, 2003) [pagination not yet available]. There are scattered examples of such department-based courses in several institutions. See, for example, UNL 206 Information and the Sciences (The University at Albany). Accessed: http://library.albany.edu/science/Syllabus.htm [March 26, 2003]; the initiative in masters level Counselor Education at California State University, Northridge. Accessed: http://www.csun.edu/edpsy/ACES/index.html [March 26, 2003]; Music 261: Music Research Techniques. University of Hawaii at Manoa. Accessed: http://www.sinclair.hawaii.edu/muse/music261.html#syllabus [March 26, 2003]; and COMM 200: Research in the Information Age. Trinity Western University. Accessed: http://www.acts.twu.ca/lbr/commsyll.htm [March 29, 2003].

33. Patrick Noon, discussing the struggle of libraries to achieve credibility and resources, writes: "Properly managed, user education can be that part of our service that actually sells the rest of the service; that activity brings the sources and services that are available to the attention of those who most need them, rather than expecting our users somehow to absorb this information by osmosis as soon as they join the institution." Patrick Noon, "Finding a Strategic Role for Information Skills in Academic Libraries," in *Information Skills in Academic Libraries*. SEDA Paper 82, 1994. Accessed: http://www.lgu.ac.uk/deliberations/seda-pubs/Noon.html [March 29, 2003].

Research and Writing and Theses–Oh My!
The Journey of a Collaboratively Taught
Graduate Research and Writing Course

Michelle Toth

SUMMARY. In the fall of 2000, the Master of Arts in Liberal Studies program at SUNY Plattsburgh added to its curriculum: MLS589 Graduate Research and Writing. This collaboratively designed course reviews research skills and strategies, examines writing style, and outlines the process for formal research proposals for graduate students. While the original collaboration and design process of this course are in itself remarkable, the continued growth and evolution of this course is the truly dynamic aspect of this collaboration. This article outlines the journey of this evolution, focusing on how continuing collaboration between an administrator, thesis advisor, and an instruction librarian is shaping the course. It takes a semester-by-semester look at the issues that came up and the solutions that were found and put into practice. These issues include: addressing the needs of distance learning students by moving to a Web-based format, rearranging the sequence of the course to facilitate the development of students' research topics and projects, and the revision of course assessment tools to monitor the changes

Michelle Toth is an Instruction Librarian, Plattsburgh State University's Feinberg Library, 2 Draper Avenue, Plattsburgh, NY 12901 (E-mail: tothmm@plattsburgh.edu).

[Haworth co-indexing entry note]: "Research and Writing and Theses–Oh My! The Journey of a Collaboratively Taught Graduate Research and Writing Course." Toth, Michelle. Co-published simultaneously in *The Reference Librarian* (The Haworth Information Press, an imprint of The Haworth Press, Inc.) No. 89/90, 2005, pp. 81-92; and: *Relationships Between Teaching Faculty and Teaching Librarians* (ed: Susan B. Kraat) The Haworth Information Press, an imprint of The Haworth Press, Inc., 2005, pp. 81-92. Single or multiple copies of this article are available for a fee from The Haworth Document Delivery Service [1-800-HAWORTH, 9:00 a.m. - 5:00 p.m. (EST). E-mail address: docdelivery@haworthpress.com].

Digital Object Identifier: 10.1300/J120v43n89_06

made in the course. Through shared responsibility and collaborative processes, the course benefits and continues to evolve and improve. *[Article copies available for a fee from The Haworth Document Delivery Service: 1-800-HAWORTH. E-mail address: <docdelivery@haworthpress.com> Website: <http://www.HaworthPress.com> © 2005 by The Haworth Press, Inc. All rights reserved.]*

KEYWORDS. Collaboration, graduate students, Web-based course, assessment

The literature of collaboration, both in the field of library science and elsewhere, is littered with lists and attributes of what it takes to create collaboration, what is needed to sustain collaboration, and/or the benefits that may come from collaborative efforts. While many (such as Cook, Davis, Dorner, Morreale, Muronaga, Raspa and Russell) vary in their wording there are several common elements among them. The one item most consistently identified as key to collaboration is that of shared goals. Other common elements found throughout the literature include: planning (curriculum and structure), collegiality (mutual trust and respect), shared workload and decision-making, administrative support, and communication (dialog, listening and networking). Other elements have also been voiced, but less universally so. These include such things as: leadership, a mutually beneficial relationship, well-matched collaborators, creativity (synergy and generating ideas) and resources (time, budget, etc.).

I was not aware of all these lists and attributes until well after my foray into a collaboratively taught course. In hindsight, and as I find myself telling the story of my involvement in a collaboratively designed and taught course, it is easy to see these elements at work. It has been said that in the literature of collaboration the "discussion about the quality of process of the relationship generally remains secondary to discussion of the resulting product" (Raspa, 4). I hope in this article, with the help of the list of attributes noted above, to present a narrative that involves both an outline of the product, and to provide my perspective on the processes and relationships in this teaching collaboration.

THE MASTER OF ARTS IN LIBERAL STUDIES PROGRAM AT PLATTSBURGH STATE UNIVERSITY

Plattsburgh State University, part of the State University of New York (SUNY) system, has 5,500 undergraduates and 780 graduate students. Approximately 75 students are currently enrolled and actively taking classes in the Master of Arts in Liberal Studies (MALS) program.

The Master's in Liberal Studies is designed to be a flexible program that will meet the individual educational and professional needs of its students. Seventy-five percent of enrollment in the program consists of returning adult students. A survey has been conducted by the MALS program to get a better demographic snapshot of our students, but their characteristics are perhaps best summed up by John Holmes when he writes: "Their remarkable heterogeneity makes a complete definition of the re-entry student difficult or misleading. We can, however, say that they are, by and large, adults between the ages of twenty-four and sixty-five, generally working, many married and with children in school, and returning to higher education after an absence of two to forty-five years" (129). The MALS survey has been able to identify that a majority of our students, approximately 60%, are currently employed in education, government and health-care professions and that about 90% of our students work full-time.

BIRTH OF A COLLABORATION

The Dean of Lifelong Learning, Dr. Janet Worthington, whose office oversees the MALS program, and the MALS thesis advisor, Dr. Kevin O'Neill, had been monitoring a decline in graduation rates for the program. The MALS program is the one Masters program on campus that still requires a thesis. Other programs over the years have opted for cumulative tests or projects. Janet and Kevin had identified the thesis component of the program as the primary obstacle for many students. The MLS590 Thesis course was the student's final class and the beginning of their theses. Students worked with Kevin in MLS590 for one semester and then were given one additional semester of access to campus services in order to complete their theses. Of the students who did not complete their theses in these two semesters, there were a growing number who would never finish. Even if students had passed all their other courses, the incomplete thesis would prevent them from earning their degrees. A similar set of problems had been identified by Diana Cunningham and Deborah Viola concerning students in a master's program for public health at New York Medical College. Much like Janet and Kevin they had found that "students often began the process too late; forms were incomplete; research was not always focused; APA format was often ignored; and students were so time constrained that the discussion sections of the theses were underdeveloped" (Cunningham, 331).

Something needed to be done to reverse this trend. The idea was to create a new course–a prerequisite to MLS590. This new one-credit course would be a preparatory semester for the thesis. It would ensure that students had the basic writing and research skills and provide an overview of the components of a thesis and start students in the process of selecting a topic and formulating research questions. This new course would give students a running start for the work to be done in MLS590. It would extend the time that students would be thinking, writing and researching their topics. It would also give them increased access to services available from the library and computer labs, as well as another semester to receive instruction, guidance and feedback on their progress. The learning objectives for this new course are at the heart of this collaboration along with the paired goal of coordinated support to help our graduate students complete quality theses.

I was approached to be part of this project after the problem had been identified and the creation of a new course had been decided upon by Janet and Kevin. The formal inclusion of a librarian as part of a team supporting graduate students working on their theses is not a new idea. Librarian involvement with students conducting graduate level research has been shown to provide "several benefits, including more completions, more timely completions, higher quality research, better information literacy skills and improved research collections" (Bruce, 110).

As a new instruction librarian, the idea of becoming involved with this course intrigued me for several reasons. First it would expand the library's instructional outreach to an underserved campus population. The college has a required one-credit information literacy course for undergraduates but has no formal program for our graduate students other than the course-related library instruction sessions requested by individual instructors. I also saw this as an opportunity to network and connect with people from different areas of the college. In my first year most of my energies had been devoted to familiarizing myself with the people and services in my own division of the college; now, near the end of my first year, was the ideal time to start reaching out. Participating in this project would also offer a way to broaden my teaching skills with a new audience and in a new format. Finally, I would explore and engage in the areas of scholarship concerning graduate students, returning adult students, teaching collaborations and assessment.

By taking on this challenge and participating in this newly forming collaboration I could simultaneously accomplish several professional and career goals. I could make a significant contribution to the instructional program at Plattsburgh State University, diversify my campus networking and service commitments, enhance my teaching skills and delve into new areas of research. The win/win and mutually beneficial relationships discussed in the lists of collaborative attributes proved very true for me.

The one-credit MLS589 Graduate Research and Writing course combines writing analysis, formal research proposal protocols and research skills to prepare students for work on their theses. The writing portion of the course taught by Janet requires students to analyze their writing style, critique a completed thesis, and learn the essential elements of a formal research paper. In the proposal portion of the course, taught by Kevin, students develop their topics, formalize their research questions and draft their Committee on the Protection of Human Subjects (COPHS) applications. In the research portion I teach students to familiarize themselves with the tools and services of the library and to begin the process of collecting and critically analyzing their research sources in an annotated bibliography.

Janet, Kevin and I each bring very different skills and experiences to the course and we all actively contributed to the course's creation and design. The process of working in collaboration to create this course was amazingly easy. This is not to say that there weren't numerous issues and aspects of the course that we needed to discuss and debate. On the contrary, every aspect of the course was reviewed by all of us together but we were able to quickly develop good communication and shared decision-making processes. We never set any formal rules about how decisions would be made, but through discussions and creative problem solving we were able to design the first semester of the course. We happily discovered that we were well-matched collaborators. The collegiality that can be found in general on this campus and the mutual respect for the different strengths we all bring to the collaboration has been key to this successful working relationship.

SEMESTER 1–FALL 2000

In the planning stages Janet, Kevin and I often discussed the interconnectedness of the different concepts and skills that we would be teaching. For example, we felt it essential that students first understand the role and purpose of the literature review in a thesis before we could successfully talk to them about their approaches to researching their topics. In our first semester the intersection of inter-related content and three instructors with different areas of expertise led to a schedule of overlapping instructors and course content.

Like the MLS590 thesis course the MLS589 class size was capped at 15 students. We decided that the course would meet for two hours once every other week. The longer class time gave us more flexibility. There was time for more than one instructor to work with the students in each class session. This enabled instructors to emphasize the connections between the different skill areas each was focusing on. The schedule was set such that the primary focus for that day would determine where the students met–in a computer classroom for the research portions, and in regular classrooms for the writing and proposal sessions. In addition, whether another instructor was scheduled to talk to the class that day or not, he or she usually appeared at the beginning of the class to pick up or return assignments. The goal for the course was a fully and seamlessly integrated interdisciplinary approach. This plan, however, was perhaps a bit ambitious. The complex nature of the course, instructor and room schedule seemed to compete with our goals to clarify the thesis process.

At the end of the first semester, along with the standardized anonymous course assessment, we had a conversation with the students at our last class meeting. A small group of adult graduate students are pretty vocal about their expectations for their education. This conversation later helped to clarify statements made by students in the course assessment (which we read after grades were submitted). The conversation also provided an opportunity to look at some course details that were not included in the course's general assessment.

After the course was completed Janet, Kevin and I met and discussed both the anonymous surveys and the conversation we had with our first group of students. Based on student feedback and our own assessments of how the course went, we modified the course. First, we simplified the course's organization by dividing it into three distinct sections: writing, research, and thesis proposal, each taught separately. Although we were attached to the interconnectedness of the areas we were teaching, we realized that separating them would simplify the course structure and would better facilitate our students' learning. Each of us would still be tying the skills and concepts to the overall goal of completing a thesis. We felt comfortable making this change because we had had the opportunity to spend the first semester becoming familiar with each other's content and teaching styles.

The second change was standardization of a citation style format for the thesis bibliographies. The MALS program as a whole does not have a specific citation format agreed upon by its faculty. Based on the student's feedback from the first semester, MLA was adopted as the format to be taught in this course and used in the thesis. With these course revisions we entered into the second semester of the course.

SEMESTER 2–SPRING 2001

The schedule change, along with a revised course Web page that provided a detailed class schedule, appeared to help the course run more smoothly in the second semester. While some structural elements of the course had been revised, the goals and objectives remained the same: to sharpen students' writing and research skills, to introduce them to the elements of a thesis and to help them begin the process of drafting necessary proposals and applications for a thesis. The overarching goal remained the commitment to helping students complete their theses in a timely manner.

Separating the course into three separate sections affected the course and the collaboration a couple of different ways. First the communication between Janet, Kevin and me diminished somewhat. This may be attributed in part to the fact that so much more needed to be discussed and agreed upon in the initial semester of the course while it was still being shaped and designed. We were also less physically present together in the course the second time around. We all appeared for the first meeting of the course to introduce ourselves and outline the syllabus and course goals. Otherwise, seeing one another in the class was rare. Kevin came to my first class as a guest speaker to outline his expectations as the thesis advisor about the literature review portion of their theses. But while the amount of face-to-face communication was reduced, we moved more to e-mail and maintained the same quality of discussion and decision-making about the course and our students. We held both pre- and post-semester meetings to discuss issues and make any necessary changes. These meetings have become standard for us in preparing and reviewing the course each time we teach.

Along with the change in format also came a change in the student evaluations for the course. We created a course survey with four distinct sections. The first section asked questions specifically about the course and its objectives as a whole. The other three sections addressed questions on the individual sections of the course we each taught. Each instructor was able to write the questions for his/her own section to address whatever specific elements they were interested in assessing.

The sectioning of the course made each of us more individually autonomous within the course. I am grateful that the first semester allowed me to interact a great deal with Janet and Kevin in the classroom. I learned a lot about their expectations for the course and our students. However, being solely responsible for a set number of classes also has its benefits. Any self-consciousness I felt about teaching in front of Janet and Kevin as two experienced senior faculty members was reduced by this new arrangement. I also felt more confident in exploring different teaching approaches and following up my students' questions knowing that I didn't have to worry about running late and going into someone else's teaching time.

SEMESTER 3–FALL 2001

In each of the first two semesters of the course there were at least one or two students who were distance-learning students. Usually they were students at our satellite site at a regional community college. The course was offered only on the main campus with no plans to accommodate distance-learning students. In the first two semesters students identified themselves as distance-learners and each of the instructors worked with them through a combination of e-mail, voice-mail and snail-mail. It was hardly the ideal way to meet our distance-learning students' needs.

At the end of the second semester Janet proposed that we move the course to the Web to address distance-learning. She was already teaching a course through the SUNY Learning Network, the SUNY-wide online course system, and loving it. Her proposal made good sense. An asynchronous Web course would better facilitate our distance-learning students, and it would allow for a more flexible schedule for all of our students. It would also allow all the instructors to "look into" the course whenever we wanted to, to see what was going on and respond to questions pertinent to our subject expertise.

Moving to a Web-based course clearly would offer a great deal more flexibility for both students and teachers and the added features of online discussions and grading could really facilitate our teaching. But the idea of being an online instructor was a bit worrying. My experience as a student in an online course the year before was not ideal. (Apparently I am more of an auditory learner than I thought.) My online student experience made me think hard about becoming an online teacher. (For a brief review of some of the issues of online teaching and learning I recommend Greg Kearsley's article "Is Online Learning for Everybody?") While I did not see it mentioned on any of the lists about the attributes of collaboration, I have realized that collaboration also means compromise and sometimes stretching our own comfort levels.

To prepare for the Web course we each participated in the SUNY Learning Network training over the summer and created our online course. The second semester segmented course design fit very nicely with the structure of modules in the Web course. We offered an "icebreaker" module in which students introduced themselves and gave their initial thoughts about what they were interested in for their thesis topics. The class then was broken down into the three sections with two modules each for writing, research, and proposals.

We were also able to transfer our assessment tool to the online environment. We made a few modifications by adding questions about how the Web course worked for our students. The switch to the online environment was generally well received and the responses to the survey questions about the course's goals remained similar to those from the on-campus sections. One suggestion made in this semester was that the research modules and the thesis proposal modules be reversed. The current sequence was writing, research and thesis proposals. Students started out with an idea for a topic, went through the writing modules, began their research on the topic and then met with Kevin in the final two modules to formalize their proposals. At this point some students either modified their topics significantly or decided to change them outright. Students then found that they would have to go back and begin new lines of research. Drafting proposals with Kevin before beginning their research would minimize the possibility that students would need to start their research all over again.

SEMESTER 4–SPRING 2002

The course remained on the Web and the research and thesis proposal modules were rearranged based on the students' feedback from the previous semester. This re-arrangement of the modules did minimize the number of students who had to go back and begin research anew because they had decided to change topics. This switch, however, did not solve everything. We then got students who decided after they started their research that not enough information was available and would go back to Kevin and modify their topics. We have decided that keeping the order: writing, proposal and research, makes the most sense and results in the least amount of work for those students who do want to change or modify their topics.

When we decided to move the course to the Web we agreed that this would be the only way the course was going to be taught. As you can imagine, this received mixed reviews from MALS students. Many, because of distance or schedule, loved the asynchronous Web environment. A few others, particularly those not very comfortable with technology, bemoaned the unavailability of this as a regular face-to-face course. While I had been able overcome my apprehensions about teaching online, I sympathized with the students who were dissatisfied with a completely Web-based experience. I decided to add what I call the "research consultation," a component that I have continued into the current semester. At about the mid-point of the two research modules, students are asked to set up in-person (if they lived near by) or by phone (if they lived at a distance) interviews with me to talk about their research. This gives them an opportunity to ask any questions or voice any concerns about their work thus far. It is also a great way to make personal contact and to get to know the students better. After this meeting some students are more willing to contact me when they have questions. During the consultation I remind students that even after they complete MLS589 they can still contact me when they have questions or need assistance with their thesis bibliographies.

REACHING OUR GOALS

Assessment has played a significant part in the continuing revisions and improvements to this course. Almost all revisions were initiated by students' evaluations and comments. Our assessments have also been used to document the success of the course. Students have been asked to respond to the statement, "I feel that this class has allowed me to make significant progress on my thesis project," in the student survey at the end of the course. The replies to this question best demonstrate our students' thoughts on the impact of the course. On a four-point scale, responses to this question average a 3.72.

In addition to the data we get from course surveys we have also been tracking our MLS589 students as they go on with their thesis work. Since we need at least a two-semester horizon to track the graduation rate, we have been able to follow the progress of the students from the course's first two semesters. For comparison, we first tracked students in the MLS590 thesis course for the three semesters prior to offering the MLS589 course. The average completion rate of the thesis within two semesters for this group of students was 52.31%. Seven students from our first semester went on and took the MLS590 thesis course. Of those seven, five completed their theses in two semesters for a completion rate of 71%. Data from our second group students is incomplete at the moment. Five students took the thesis course in the fall of 2001. Two students completed their theses in one semester, the other three have not yet finished. One student from the second semester of MLS589 has waited to take the MLS590 course in Spring 2003. We will continue to track our student's progress as one of the measures for meeting our goals.

Improving the quality of theses has been stated as a goal of MLS589 from the beginning, but no specific research has yet been conducted to measure this. Copies of completed theses are currently archived in the MALS program and will be easily available when we decide to pursue this aspect of assessment. Kevin, in his capacity as the thesis advisor, has said anecdotally that he has noted improved quality of the work produced by our students.

THE FUTURE OF THE COURSE AND THE COLLABORATION

Many collaborative courses or projects have a short shelf life. Issues such as administrative support, a changing cast of characters and the simple desire to keep a collaboration alive in an academic world full of teaching commitments, committee work and research all contribute to limit the lifespan of collaborative efforts.

I have no doubt that the significant support for the MLS589 course received from Dean Janet Worthington had a great deal to do with getting this course off the ground and ensuring its continuance. Through her efforts as both an administrator and an energetic participant of our teaching collaboration we were able to take this from an experimental course to one that is now officially "on the books" as a requirement and prerequisite for the MLS590 thesis course. Her enthusiasm has clearly been a driving force for the course. I greeted, with sadness and a touch of apprehension, her announcement that she would retire at the end of the Spring 2003 semester. Her contributions will be missed.

Kevin and I have agreed to continue our participation of the course. Janet has been able to recruit a replacement for her portion of the course. In the Fall 2003 semester the writing specialist from the campus learning center will be working with us to guide the writing of our graduate students in MLS589. This change heralds a new chapter for both the course and the collaboration; it is my hope that this new tradition of collaborative teaching, course evolution and student accomplishment will continue.

REFERENCES

Bruce, Christine. "Faculty-Librarian Partnerships in Australian Higher Education: Critical Dimensions." *Reference Services Review.* 29:2 (2001): 106-115.

Cook, Doug. "Creating Connections: A Review of the Literature," in Dick Raspa and Dane Ward, eds. *The Collaborative Imperative: Librarians and Faculty Working Together in the Information Universe.* American Library Association, Chicago, IL, 2000, 19-38.

Cunningham, Diana and Deborah Viola. "Collaboration to Teach Graduate Students How to Write More Effective Theses." *Journal of the Medical Library Association.* 90:3 (2002): 331-334.

Davis, James R. "Chapter 4–When Faculty Work in Teams: Learning from the Research on Groups and Teams," in *Interdisciplinary Courses and Team Teaching: New Arrangements for Learning.* Oryx, Phoenix, AZ, 1995, 76-99.

Dorner, Jennifer, Susan E. Taylor and Kay Hodson-Carlton. "Faculty-Librarian Collaboration for Nursing Information Literacy: A Tiered Approach." *Reference Services Review.* 29:2 (2001): 132-140.

Holmes, John W. "Just in Case, Just in Time, Just for You: User Education for the Re-Entry Student," in *Teaching the New Library to Today's Users: Reaching International, Minority, Senior Citizens, Gay/Lesbian, First-Generation, At-Risk, Graduate and Returning Students and Distance Learners.* Neal-Schuman, New York, 2000, 127-14.

Kearsley, Greg. "Is Online Learning for Everybody?" *Educational Technology.* (January-Febuary 2002): 41-44.

Morreale, Sherwyn P. and Carla B. Howery. "Interdisciplinary Collaboration: Down with the Silos and Up with Engagement." *American Association for Higher Education.* www.aahe.org/interdisciplinary.pdf.

Muronaga, Karen and Violet Harada. "The Art of Collaboration." *Teacher Librarian.* 27:1 (1999): 9.

Raspa, Dick and Dane Ward. "Listening for Collaboration: Faculty and Librarians Working Together," in Dick Raspa and Dane Ward, eds. *The Collaborative Imperative: Librarians and Faculty Working Together in the Information Universe.* American Library Association, Chicago, IL, 2000, 1-18.

Russell, Shayne. "Teachers and Librarians: Collaborative Relationships." *ERIC Digest.* (August 2000).

Library Research Project
for First-Year Engineering Students:
Results from Collaboration
by Teaching and Library Faculty

Rachel Callison
Dan Budny
Kate Thomes

SUMMARY. This article will discuss three years of collaboration between the Freshman Engineering Program and the Engineering Library of the University Library System at the University of Pittsburgh. This collaboration has resulted in a library research project that is integrated into the freshman curriculum. The project ultimately provides the students with a research structure for presentations in an annual mock professional conference. The mission of the Freshman Engineering Program's academic and advising components is to create a first-year experience that promotes the student's continued pursuit of an engineer-

Rachel Callison (E-mail: callison@pitt.edu) is Reference/Public Services Librarian, Bevier Engineering Library, Dan Budny (E-mail: budny@pitt.edu) is Academic Director of Freshman Programs, School of Engineering, and Kate Thomes (E-mail: kthomes@pitt.edu) is Head, Bevier Engineering Library, all at the University of Pittsburgh, Pittsburgh, PA.

[Haworth co-indexing entry note]: "Library Research Project for First-Year Engineering Students: Results from Collaboration by Teaching and Library Faculty." Callison, Rachel, Dan Budny, and Kate Thomes. Co-published simultaneously in *The Reference Librarian* (The Haworth Information Press, an imprint of The Haworth Press, Inc.) No. 89/90, 2005, pp. 93-106; and: *Relationships Between Teaching Faculty and Teaching Librarians* (ed: Susan B. Kraat) The Haworth Information Press, an imprint of The Haworth Press, Inc., 2005, pp. 93-106. Single or multiple copies of this article are available for a fee from The Haworth Document Delivery Service [1-800-HAWORTH, 9:00 a.m. - 5:00 p.m. (EST). E-mail address: docdelivery@haworthpress.com].

Digital Object Identifier: 10.1300/J120v43n89_07

ing degree through commitment to clearly understood and self-declared goals. The goal for the Engineering Library is to introduce library research as a necessary skill-set for successful engineers. The successful outcome of all of these goals requires the collaboration between "teaching" faculty and "library" faculty and results in better prepared, more focused students. Developing and integrating a library research project into the freshman engineering academic curriculum is a significant opportunity for library instruction, and the approach demonstrated here may be transferable to other disciplines. *[Article copies available for a fee from The Haworth Document Delivery Service: 1-800-HAWORTH. E-mail address: <docdelivery@haworthpress.com> Website: <http://www.HaworthPress.com> © 2005 by The Haworth Press, Inc. All rights reserved.]*

KEYWORDS. Curriculum integrated library instruction, collaboration, engineering education, freshman

INTRODUCTION

Curriculum integration of library instruction is essential in establishing its importance in the minds of students. As Ken Haycock points out, "students do not use instructional programs that are offered on a voluntary basis and removed from classroom instruction; they are too busy and do not see any immediate need. If we are serious about implementing information literacy programs, we need to start with the construction of assignments and the instruction provided for their effective completion. That means that we start with faculty colleagues."

Some (of the) basic principles of learning theory that focus on learner-centered education include:

- learning has more meaning if it comes from experience
- learners are most ready to learn when they have a real-life need to know something
- and learners want to be able to make a practical application to their lives of what they learn (Knowles 1980).

So, successful learning occurs when what is to be learned is made pertinent to the learner. This relevancy is especially true to learning library resources because the importance of these resources is not readily apparent to the student. For any resource to appear as important or useful, its presentation must be integrated into the "need to know" schema of the learner.

"Since the 1970s, many educators and librarians have advocated incorporating information literacy into the curriculum, but this is much easier said than accomplished. Comprehensively incorporating information literacy instruction into college and university courses takes a commitment on the part of library professionals, the teaching faculty, and the university administration" (Dorner, Taylor & Hodson-Carlton 2001). Once the concept of curriculum integrated library instruction is accepted by teaching and library faculty, the benefits of instructional collaboration are numerous. Faculty can discover the extent of what the library and librarians have to offer their students. Library faculty can provide more effective service since they have an earlier awareness of research and assignment needs. Although these are significant benefits, the most important benefit of collaboration is the creation and presentation of a relevant, cohesive learning environment for the student.

Each institution, department, or library will have different approaches to collaborative efforts based on their respective environments. A study of pedagogical approaches by Leckie and Fullerton (April 1999) points out that "the acculturation of librarians is quite opposite to that of (teaching) faculty. Librarians tend to place their client's needs first and foremost and seek to work collaboratively, while (most) faculty place their own research above all else and seek to work independently." But the study also noted that medical science and engineering faculty believe a pedagogical emphasis should be placed on critical thinking and research skills and voiced a need to have the learning of these skills integrated into the curriculum (Leckie and Fullerton January 1999).

Understanding that there can be differing approaches to the integration of information literacy into the curriculum can help us to see why librarians and faculty may have difficulty agreeing on an appropriate course of action, even though both groups wish to accomplish similar goals. A good starting point for instructional collaboration is to identify the learning objectives of faculty and of librarians and to begin to design the curriculum with both sets of objectives in mind. An article by Black, Crest and Volland (2001) addresses many of the issues surrounding relationship building with faculty and states that "although faculty supply the content from their discipline, it is the librarian who shapes the research questions and teaches the student the necessary skill in finding the answers."

The main key to any type of collaboration is the ability of the involved parties to consistently communicate their respective goals and objectives throughout the planning process. "An important factor in the success of any collaboration is the commitment to increased communication. Students need to receive compatible messages from the professor and librarian. Working together, a professor-librarian team can provide the assistance needed to guide students successfully through the research process" (Stein and Lamb 1998). Thus, each part of the team needs to be aware of the others' goals and coordinate efforts when it comes to the dissemination of the assignments and outcomes to the students.

COLLABORATIVE EFFORTS
OF THE BEVIER ENGINEERING LIBRARY

Collaboration between the School of Engineering freshman academic program and the library at the University of Pittsburgh began in Fall 1996, with the design of a research project in which students investigated a high profile engineering failure. Goals of this assignment included raising awareness of engineering's role in society, learning how to use library resources, and learning how to write a technical paper (Thomes, Cornell, Gottfried 1997). From the library's perspective, this provided valuable interaction with the students and an opportunity to expose them to the library in the context of a specific assignment. However, the project stood in relative isolation from the rest of the freshman curriculum, and the relevance of library skills to practicing engineers may not have been clear. The School of Engineering's Mentoring Program also began in 1996 as an effort to ease the transition from high school to the university by creating teams of freshmen headed by junior and senior level engineering students. A main objective of the Mentoring Program is to assist each student in making a smooth transition from high school to college (Budny 2001). So, although collaboration had occurred between the academic and advising programs and between the academic and library programs, it wasn't until 2000 that all three were fully integrated.

In 2000, the new Freshman Programs Director indicated that he was interested in going outside the traditional classroom model with this course. Even after restructuring their curriculum, the freshman studies program leaders realized that a traditional engineering problem solving course would not provide enough opportunities for written and oral presentation assignments and research. There was still a need for students to develop written and oral communication skills within the curriculum.

Thus, the Freshman Director proposed that a simulated professional conference be held in April 2001 as the culminating event of freshman year activities.

PLANNING AND DESIGNING
THE LIBRARY RESEARCH PROJECT

In August 2001, the Project Team met several times to discuss a design for a Library Research Project that would meet the objectives of the Academic Program, the Advising Program and the Engineering Library. Emphasis was placed on tailoring the research activities to meet our multiple objectives. Additionally, the Library Research Project would provide the background and training that would prepare these students for the mock Sustainability Conference the following spring.

Academic and Advising Objectives

The freshman programs director expressed the wish that the Library Research Project should support the academic and advising goal of promoting the students' continued pursuit of an engineering degree. The following academic objectives were incorporated into the project:

- introducing students to the necessary computer tools to meet the needs of their future departments,
- introducing the concept of teamwork, and
- improving the communication skills of the students.

The director also wanted to emphasize the advising objective of aiding students to identify their major by the end of their first year.

Library Objectives

The librarians worked to ensure that the curriculum design would address established engineering education goals including the ABET (Accreditation Board for Engineering and Technology) guideline stating that engineering graduates should be able to teach themselves new concepts and apply information to new and unfamiliar situations. Information literacy seemed an appropriate skill set to help address this goal (Nerz and Weiner 2001). The University Library System provides access to ever increasing collections of electronic and print resources. As a result, first-year engineering students are presented with a modern academic research environment that can be overwhelming. Consequently, and unfortunately, it is common to hear junior and senior students say they do not know how to conduct research within the literature of engineering. Engineering is an increasingly interdisciplinary field. Real world problems that future engineers will face will require them to combine knowledge and understanding from several fields outside their specific area of engineering and outside of engineering itself. While it is not reasonable to expect engineers to have mastery over all subjects, it is reasonable to expect them to be able to find and analyze relevant information as needed.

Another set of educational goals comes from what employers expect of recent graduates. According to Rodrigues, "Corporations expect their newly hired engineers to be able to 'hit the ground running.'" He also states that "Engineering students should be departing the university with the following proficiencies:

- basic knowledge of how a typical engineering library is organized and familiarity with general and engineering-specific reference books,
- working knowledge of the nature and usefulness of a wide range of journals relevant to (their) field,
- awareness of the professional associations that support their engineering specialty, and
- the rudiments of searching relevant online sources."

The challenge set before us was how to create a curriculum that could satisfy all of our goals and objectives.

Project Design

The Project Team agreed that the overall theme of the Library Research Project for the fall term should focus on the student's exploration of an area of engineering that interested them. Frequently, incoming freshman have misconceptions about what engineers really do and how varied engineering careers can be. Research into the realities of engineering careers at this early stage would help students make informed decisions about their educational goals. This theme addresses the advising premise that students with clarity of purpose have improved motivation and commitment to the engineering program.

From the Library's perspective, this theme allows introduction of a range of databases, resources, and concepts in a student centered environment. As mentioned previously, students learn better when they understand the purpose of the exercise. The Library Research Project was designed to motivate the students on two fronts. Not only would they earn course credit, but they would also be able to gather information to assist them in making important educational and career decisions. The project would introduce students to the technical and research skills they would need for the Spring Conference as well as serve as a trial run for using a prescribed format to write a technical paper and presenting that paper to a group of their peers using PowerPoint software.

The Engineering Librarians felt that the assignments should expose students to resources that they would need throughout their undergraduate program. They should also present information literacy skills that will continue to serve them as professionals by introducing them to library resources, the research process, and critical thinking skills needed to analyze the validity and utility of information. Introducing library skills during the first semester demonstrates the fundamental importance of these skills in engineering education.

PROJECT STRUCTURE

The Library Research Project was incorporated into Engineering 0011, a required three-credit course and Engineering 0080, a required non-credit course. A portion of Engineering 0011 is taught interactively in a cooperative learning environment where students work in teams to solve the course requirements. The rest of the course is taught in a lecture environment with emphasis on the relationship between engineering sciences and engineering design.

Although Engineering 0080 (Freshman Seminar) is a non-credit course, the course is required and students are graded pass/fail based on attendance and participation. During the term, students meet with their respective junior and senior mentors once a week for an organized class. Groups are capped at 15 students per mentor in order to establish a close bond. Mentors and students are encouraged to meet outside of class for informal teambuilding activities.

The time frame of the assignments was devised so that the students would have their final papers done before they left for the Thanksgiving recess. Their oral presentations would be presented when they arrived back from the break. The students would have three weeks to write their papers, preceded by three weeks to conduct the relevant research. This meant that the project needed to be introduced six weeks prior to the Thanksgiving recess.

To meet that schedule the librarians designed four assignments, one due each week for the first three weeks and the fourth (writing the paper) with a three-week deadline. The assignments were designed to guide students through an information gathering process and a time management process as well. Having weekly deadlines would (1) keep the students on a schedule, i.e., no waiting until the night before to write the final paper, (2) allow them to progressively gather information and build their research skills, and (3) assist the mentors by limiting the occurrence of unrelated questions, thus enabling them to focus their feedback to the students.

Students handed in the first three individual assignments of the Library Research Project to their mentors via their non-credit Engineering 0080 (Freshman Seminar) course. The fourth assignment, the final paper, comprised 15 percent of the student's grade in their for-credit Engineering 0011 course. This structure allowed the students to build up research skills during the first three assignments in a low-risk environment before completing their fourth assignment, the final paper, which was a significant part of their final grade.

The librarians met with all of the mentors in order to explain the purpose and structure of the project. Mentors were given the responsibility of providing feedback and assistance with the research project, for grading each of the first three library research components, and for assisting faculty with the evaluation of the final papers and presentations.

In order to clearly present what was expected of the students, and to limit any room for interpretation, the assignments were highly structured. From the advising perspective, this would ease the transition from high school work to the more independent requirements of higher education. A survey by Valentine (1999) indicates that (research) stress levels of students is decreased when the graded library assignment introduces them to the range of resources they will use for their final paper. Students seemed to take more ownership of the process and appreciate the research experience more. This survey also revealed that allowing students to have some say in topic choice increases their personal commitment to the library assignment. Due to large class size, 380 students, this intensive structuring also made the grading of the assignments more manageable for the mentors.

ASSIGNMENT CONTENT

An overview and rationale for the Library Research Project was provided to the students along with a dateline of when each component would be due. Each research component included a statement of purpose (or learning objective) so the students would understand why they were doing this work. Research/Resource Guides for each assignment were designed to supply the students with additional guidance to the resources they would need to consult for each assignment.

The first research assignment was designed to introduce students to various engineering professional societies as a way to help them explore engineering as a career. Advising goals were being met by having freshmen investigate the information provided by professional societies and asking them to think about "What types of things do 'X-type' of engineers do?" and "Is that what I want to do?" This assignment was Web-based to capitalize on students' tendency to use the Web first for research, but focused on the critical thinking process by asking students to carefully analyze Web sites for point of view/purpose, authority, accuracy, and currency. Students compared non-engineering Web sites to engineering society Web sites using stated evaluation criteria.

In assignment two, the concept of "What do engineers do?" was further explored by having students use resources that dealt with career and job information specific to their chosen area. Reference was made to the first assignment with regard to using professional society Web sites as a source for employment information. Reviewing job postings of companies that employ engineers introduced the students to the types of skill sets employers of engineers look for, thus meeting academic and advising goals by asking students to consider "What courses am I going to need to take in order to obtain these skills . . . and find a job?" Asking students to consider using the company information they found to identify a service or product as a topic for their conference paper allows them to get a jump on research gathering and strategies for the spring term.

The third assignment required students to use electronic indexes to find articles on a topic of interest related to their area of engineering, begin the process of differentiating between an "academic" or "scholarly" journal article versus a "trade" or "popular" magazine article, and analyze the information that they found. Academic goals were met by having them research a specific topic and write about their findings.

Students were asked to submit assignments two and three using the prescribed format that they would need to use for the final paper. Having these two "trial runs" allowed the students to concentrate on the content, rather than the format, of their final paper.

The fourth, and final, assignment was designed to assist them with: pulling together the information they had gathered from the previous three assignments, finding additional research materials to supplement their existing resources, and writing their final technical paper. The students were to prepare an oral (PowerPoint) presentation based on the material from their paper and present it to their mentor groups. Since the students' spring term conference paper and presentation would be based on these same criteria, we felt that this reiteration would solidify the research process for them.

IMPLEMENTATION

During the fifth week of the Fall Term, a 45-minute presentation by the Engineering Library was delivered to each of the six Engineering 0011 sections. All of the Engineering faculty who teach these sections were present during the Library's presentation. The presentation focused on the concept that all engineers, regardless of their area of interest, are problem solvers. In order for engineers to solve problems they have to make "informed" decisions, which involves knowing how to gather information and then analyze it. This process of gathering and analysis was offered to the students as a definition of research. It was explained that the Library Research Project is an introduction to the research process and would assist them with the "challenge" of determining what area of engineering they wished to pursue, as well as preparing for the Sustainability Conference in the spring term.

The Library Research Project Overview and Outline handouts were distributed and discussed during the library's presentation. It was explained that a detailed assignment handout and a related research guide would be distributed to them during their weekly mentor group meetings.

Toward the end of the presentation, a general overview of the library system at the University of Pittsburgh using the University Library System Web Site was provided. Resources and services specific to the project are emphasized such as: Instruction sessions on using PITTCat (online catalog), Writing Center location and hours, and the electronic Engineering Subject Guide to Resources. Students were encouraged to come to the Engineering Library for assistance because staff and librarians are there to provide guidance and support.

The Engineering Librarians met with the mentors in a separate session to discuss the library research project and address any of their questions or concerns. Since the mentors would assist with grading the freshman students' weekly assignments, final paper, and oral presentation, the project leaders wanted to insure that the mentors were comfortable with the project and understood the referral process with regard to questions they could not answer. Within the Engineering Library, the librarians and staff also met to discuss the project. During the term, a binder containing the Library Research Project was kept at the front desk. This way, all of the library staff were familiar with the project and were aware of which assignment the students would be working on in any given week, as well as the resources students were being asked to access and use

The Academic Program Director posted all of the course materials, including the Library Research Project, on the course Web site. To further the integration of the library research project with Engineering 0011, students were required to put the data collected in the first three library research assignments onto Web pages previously created as an assignment for that course.

SUSTAINABILITY CONFERENCE

In the spring semester, students were informed that one of the key components of the Engineering 0012 course, a continuation of the Engineering 0011 course, would be the preparation of a formal written paper for publication and presentation at a conference to be held at the end of the term. Given that the School of Engineering uses an integrated curriculum approach for their freshman courses, students were told that their papers should relate to topics covered in the fall or spring semester of their Physics, Chemistry, Calculus or Engineering classes. Additionally, they were asked to link their chosen topics to an area of engineering using the idea of sustainability in the new millennium as the common conference thread. The key idea was to expand upon the concept of curriculum integration by having students merge material from their core courses with material they had learned in their introduction to engineering seminar courses. Because of the large class size at the University of Pittsburgh (380 students), all papers were required to have two co-authors.

Throughout the spring semester, students were exposed to all aspects involved in the preparation of a formal paper for publication, including:

- responding to a call for papers,
- being notified of the acceptance of their abstracts,
- conducting the necessary research, preparing and submitting a paper for review,
- conducting a review of a fellow student's paper, and
- receiving and utilizing peer feedback to prepare a final paper.

The Engineering Library provided additional guides in the spring term for the students on how to approach the research process, along with appropriate resources for their conference paper.

OUTCOMES, FUTURE ACTIVITIES, AND CONCLUSION

As of April 2003, there have been three Annual Sustainability Conferences. This creative approach recognizes the real-world role of library resources and research skills in preparing and writing conference papers. Since the Library Research Project was not isolated from the rest of the curriculum, students saw the interrelationship of the Advising, Academic, and Library objectives. The faculty, student mentors, and support staff surrounding the students were all involved so that the students would understand the importance of the project. Through this integrated approach to instruction, students at the University of Pittsburgh are now introduced to the culture of academic research and the literature of engineering.

Since considerable energy went into the initial design and implementation of the Library Research project, a formal assessment tool to ascertain library skills has not yet been developed. However, there has been anecdotal feedback from students regarding the overall project. While doing the library research project, students indicated that they discovered:

- *"all the possibilities you open by earning a degree in engineering."*
- *"I thought all engineers were confined to doing research . . . I found many different things the Materials Science and Mechanical Engineers can do with their degrees."*
- that *"good engineers need to have good written and verbal skills."*
- that *"engineering is not an individual venture. It takes a lot of working with groups of people from similar and different disciplines of engineering to get a job done right."*

Faculty also provided feedback indicating that the project is having a positive effect. As one faculty member stated, he was "blown away by the quality of the writing of (my) students compared to previous years."

Some future goals for the library would be to design and incorporate a formal assessment tool and to design and offer smaller, hands-on sessions that relate to the research guides for students who feel the need to obtain additional guidance beyond the library's presentation and research guides.

Presenting library skills to first-year students during their first semester demonstrates the fundamental importance of these skills to their pursuit of an engineering education. All aspects of the first-year Library Project allowed students the opportunity to link the active process of conducting research and writing to sound, scientific content in the form of a conference paper. This activity also provided the instructors with an additional assessment tool outside the limits of more traditional assessment measures. Collaboration between the Freshman Academic and Advising Programs and the Engineering Library creates a student-centered learning environment that helps first-year students make informed decisions about their future education and career goals in engineering.

REFERENCES

Black, Christine, Crest, Sarah, and Volland, Mary. "Building a successful information literacy infrastructure on the foundation of librarian-faculty collaboration." *Research Strategies* 18: 3 (2001): 215-225.

Budny, Dan. "The Freshman Seminar: Assisting the Freshman Engineering Student's Transition from High School to College." *Proceedings of the 2001 American Society for Engineering Education Annual Conference.*

Dorner, Jennifer, Taylor, Susan E., and Hodson-Carlton, Kay. "Faculty-librarian collaboration for nursing information literacy: A tiered approach." *Reference Services Review* 29: 2 (2001): 132-141.

Haycock, Ken. "Information literacy as a key connector for all libraries: What all librarians can learn from teacher librarians." In D. Booker (Ed.), *Concept, challenge, conundrum: From library skills to information literacy*; Proceedings of the fourth national information literacy conference conducted by the University of South Australia Library and the Australian Library and Information Association Information Literacy and Special Interest Group, December 3-5, 1999: 25-34. Adelaide, SA: University of South Australia Library. Available at http://www.infolit.org/documents/librarians.html (March 27, 2003).

Knowles, M.S. *The Modern Practice of Adult Education: From Pedagogy to Andragogy.* (1980, rev. ed) Association Press, Wilton, CT; Follett Pub. Co., Chicago, IL.

Leckie, G. and Fullerton, A. "The Roles of Academic Librarians in Fostering a Pedagogy for Information Literacy." *ACRL Ninth Annual Conference*, Detroit, MI. April 8-11, 1999.

Leckie, G. and Fullerton, A. "Information Literacy in science and engineering undergraduate education: Faculty attitudes and pedagogical practices." *College & Research Libraries* 60:1 (January 1999): 9-30.

Nerz, Honora and Weiner, Suzanne. "Information Competencies: A Strategic Approach." *2001 ASEE Annual Conference Proceedings* [Best Conference Paper 2001].

Rodriques, Ronald. "Industry expectations of the new engineer." *Science & Technology Libraries* 19: 3/4 (2001): 179-188.

Stein, Linda and Lamb, Jane. "Not just another BI: Faculty-librarian collaboration to guide students through the research process." *Research Strategies* 16: 1 (1998): 29-39.

Thomes, Kate, Cornell, Evan and Gottfried, Byron. "Teaching Freshmen to Write Technical Reports and to Navigate the Library: A Win-Win Situation." *1997 ASEE-FIE Annual Conference Proceedings* (1997): 1557-1563.

Valentine, Barbara. "Students versus the Research Paper: What Can We Learn?" *ACRL Ninth Annual Conference*, April 8-11, 1999, Detroit, Michigan.

Librarians in the Classroom

Peggie Partello

SUMMARY. This article reports on a survey conducted by the author to determine how librarians and library directors feel about librarians teaching outside the library, i.e., in academic disciplines. The author discusses her own experience in the classroom and examines the benefits and detriments of the "professor librarian" model. She includes comments from those surveyed, and offers suggestions for further study. *[Article copies available for a fee from The Haworth Document Delivery Service: 1-800-HAWORTH. E-mail address: <docdelivery@haworthpress.com> Website: <http://www.HaworthPress.com> © 2005 by The Haworth Press, Inc. All rights reserved.]*

KEYWORDS. Librarians, academic librarians, librarian role, teaching, classroom teaching, higher education

INTRODUCTION

I have been an academic librarian for the past 20 years and have spent most of that time working in college and university libraries. Since I know I do not like routine and need to challenge myself to stay engaged,

Peggie Partello is Director, Curriculum Materials Library, Keene State College, 229 Main Street, Keene, NH, 03435-3201 (E-mail: ppartell@keene.edu).

[Haworth co-indexing entry note]: "Librarians in the Classroom." Partello, Peggie. Co-published simultaneously in *The Reference Librarian* (The Haworth Information Press, an imprint of The Haworth Press, Inc.) No. 89/90, 2005, pp. 107-120; and: *Relationships Between Teaching Faculty and Teaching Librarians* (ed: Susan B. Kraat) The Haworth Information Press, an imprint of The Haworth Press, Inc., 2005, pp. 107-120. Single or multiple copies of this article are available for a fee from The Haworth Document Delivery Service [1-800-HAWORTH, 9:00 a.m. - 5:00 p.m. (EST). E-mail address: docdelivery@haworthpress.com].

http://www.haworthpress.com/web/REF
© 2005 by The Haworth Press, Inc. All rights reserved.
Digital Object Identifier: 10.1300/J120v43n89_08

I have sought various renewal opportunities over time. I have performed a variety of jobs from reference to collection development to director. I have served on technology, general education, and many other committees. I have served on local nonprofit boards where my research and knowledge management skills were used to meet the goals of the organization and where I have set up and/or maintained libraries and archives. I have edited, indexed, presented, published, reviewed, and translated. I have enjoyed taking classes in ceramics, sociology, and Spanish at the colleges where I have worked. I have even gotten an M.B.A.

Two years ago I was asked to teach in the communications department at Keene State College, where I am employed as a full-time librarian. At first, I dismissed the idea, figuring that it was outside the scope of my library duties and, therefore, wouldn't be supported. After discussing it with the interim library director, however, I came to see the idea in a new light. He wanted the librarians to be more visible on campus and to actively participate in the life of the college. Teaching in a discipline area would be a major avenue for increased visibility.

And so I became an adjunct professor in the communications department. I taught one section of Principles of Communication in the fall semester and two sections in the spring–all during the day. At the same time, I volunteered to advise students who had not yet decided upon a major.

The benefits to me personally and professionally were enormous. I felt directly involved in meeting the mission of the college in a way that I don't feel in the library. Even though I teach library instruction and enjoy doing it, I do not get the satisfaction I did when working with students throughout the semester and seeing them learn and grow. It is difficult, if not impossible, to know if you have made a difference in only one library instruction class.

As with any venture, there are benefits and drawbacks. Here are some of the benefits I experienced:

- An increased appreciation for the work life of a typical teaching faculty member and the problems and issues they face in the classroom.
- A sense of camaraderie and mutual respect with teaching faculty.
- A new understanding of who students really are. Of course, I was aware that many of the students work full-time to fund their education, have children at home, struggle to pay the bills. As a librarian, I don't have sustained relationships with students that allow for a complete picture.

- My work as a librarian became informed by my work in the class-room.
- A different type of interaction with faculty on issues that were related to my role as a classroom teacher instead of my role as librarian.
- Inclusion in workshops about teaching and learning that were hosted by teaching faculty.
- Learning to use Blackboard in my classes. As a result, I was asked to serve on a technology committee with other teaching faculty and to present my methods of using it to the campus.

Benefits accrued to my students as well:

- They learned to use the library because library instruction was embedded throughout the course and assignments required students to use library resources.
- They felt comfortable asking me questions about doing research and locating information for other courses.
- They learned that the library is less intimidating than they had thought.

Of course, as with any venture, there were drawbacks. Here are the most noticeable:

- Some of my librarian colleagues did not regard teaching outside the library as relevant to my duties as a librarian. In fact, I was advised not to go up for tenure that year specifically because the librarians might not recognize my work as worthy of tenure, since it was outside the scope of traditional librarianship.
- While I was allotted release time to teach my classes, release time for class preparation was granted for the first semester only. I spent many hours beyond the 40 required of librarians doing work for my classes.
- Teaching faculty had spring break, a lengthy Christmas vacation, and reading days to mark papers, prepare presentations, grade quizzes and tests, update course materials, etc. As a 12-month employee, I did not have these breaks, unless I chose to use my vacation time.

The positives outweigh the negatives for me. As I thought about the experience and its impact on my librarianship, I became curious about other librarians' experiences teaching in academic disciplines and whether librarians were interested in teaching outside the typical library instruction program.

THE LITERATURE REVIEW

I performed a literature search in *Library Literature*, *ERIC*, *Academic Search Premier*, *Education Index*, and *Dissertation Abstracts*. While there are many articles and documents about library instruction and some about course-integrated library instruction, only a handful were specifically about librarians as teachers in the academic disciplines.

Yerburgh (1979, p. 441) saw evidence that librarians were "moving closer to the line of demarcation that separates the world of librarianship from the world of classroom teaching." He noted that an increasing number of librarians were entering the profession with second master's degrees and even doctorates. Many had previous classroom teaching experience, placing them in an ideal position to teach students both subject knowledge and research skills.

Leonard (1989), who wrote from his experience as a library dean and as a chief academic officer, found that librarians do not necessarily understand the nature of teaching and learning on campus simply because they are classified as faculty. While he acknowledges the range and quantity of instruction that occurs within the library, he maintains that librarians are removed from the teaching and learning experience that occurs in the traditional classroom. He offers as support his observation that, while teaching faculty often come into the library to conduct personal research and to arrange library instruction for their students, librarians rarely enter into the classroom unless specifically invited to offer a library instruction session. Much of today's research can be performed without coming into the library, although teaching faculty still interact with librarians. They do so when ordering materials, including electronic databases, for the collection; when consulting librarians regarding their areas of expertise; when serving on library advisory committees; or when planning meaningful learning experiences for their students. Librarians generally don't advise or consult teaching faculty, or enter into the business of the classroom in the same way.

Douglas (1999) points out the problem with the dual role of librarian/professor in regards to the tenure and promotion issue. She asks, "Can librarians who do not teach make effective judgments about the teaching ability of the professor librarian?" Borchuk and Bergup (1976) came to the conclusion that librarians in classroom teaching roles had a good argument for gaining faculty status if they didn't already possess it. Hall states that librarians have de jure faculty status but are not, in most cases, "real" faculty (1990, p. 104). In addition to the benefits to the librarian and the library, teaching in the disciplines accords real faculty status to librarians who engage in it.

Douglas concludes that the benefits of teaching outweigh the problems, especially the opportunity to truly get to know students better than is possible in a 50-minute library instruction session. Sabol, an academic librarian who taught an English course, agreed (1977). She found that she became "more acutely aware of student limitations and needs, administrative red tape, and faculty workload."

THE PURPOSE OF THE STUDY

The purpose of the study was to find out what librarians think about teaching in academic disciplines. I also wanted to know what librarians with such teaching experience thought were the benefits and/or detriments of teaching in academic disciplines. Finally, I wanted to know if library directors support librarians teaching in academic disciplines.

THE METHODOLOGY

I designed two surveys–one for library directors and one for librarians. I requested and received permission to post the surveys to COLLIB-L (College Libraries Section of ACRL), ILI-L Information Literacy Instruction Listserv), and LIBADMIN (Library Administration and Management).

The questions on the librarian survey were designed to elicit information about librarians' status; whether they have subject specialties; their experiences teaching in academic disciplines, if any; and if they would like to teach. The questions in the director survey were designed to elicit information about the status of librarians the directors supervise and whether they support librarians teaching in academic disciplines.

FINDINGS

Sixty-one librarians responded to the survey. Here is a summary of the findings:

- 100% taught library instruction classes
- 75.4% were faculty
- 65.6% had a subject specialty
- 45.6% have taught or currently teach a class in an academic discipline
- Of those who have not taught, 63.9% would like the opportunity
- 81% think that classroom teaching furthers the institution's mission; 6.9% think it doesn't; and 12.1% have no opinion

Librarians with teaching experience were asked to choose what they liked about the experience–contribution to professional development; improvement of teaching skills; involvement in campus life; recognition as peer by teaching faculty. "Improvement of teaching skills" ranked highest, although there was no significant difference.

Many of the librarians found teaching in a semester-long format more satisfying than library instruction because they got to know students better and were with them through the entire learning process. They also noted that it helped them gain a perspective on the life of teaching faculty that they don't get in the library. Many said their librarianship was informed because of their teaching experience, especially in reference, collection development, and library instruction. Several librarians said they appreciated the opportunity to exercise their intellectual abilities in a way that is impossible in library instruction classes.

Here are selected comments from the librarians:

- We as librarians cannot contribute to this end [developing responsible, contributing citizens] by confining ourselves to the library.
- Teaching a non-library class . . . keeps me mentally alert and thriving [and] allows me to pursue a strong personal interest.
- Any opportunity we have to participate in classroom instruction . . . can only help in raising student–and faculty–awareness of what we do as professionals.
- Dealing with designing a course from scratch, working with mainly non-traditional students, dealing with student crises, meeting grading and registrar deadlines, made me appreciate all the more the hard work and time the teaching faculty devote to their students and courses.
- I found out that my instructions for assignments are not always as clear as I had thought. This has made me more patient with students who come to the reference desk confused by what they need to do for a research assignment.

- By teaching outside the library, I feel I'm continuing the tradition of the great librarians of our past.
- We are what we are, not "wannabes" for some other discipline.
- I do experience the confusion of being regarded as not quite as serious a scholar as my discipline-based colleagues since I do not hold a doctorate, but yet am a faculty and teaching colleague.
- I have noticed that not all librarians enjoy teaching, nor do they all wish to teach. This seems to be creating somewhat of a rift in the profession.
- If I had wanted to teach academic courses as a main part of my job, I would have gotten a Ph.D.
- I liked the "power" of the classroom when I was faculty because it let me choose readings and types of writings, develop classes within the guidelines for specific courses, and experience the respect that faculty gets.

Forty-six directors responded to the survey. Here is a summary of the findings:

- 71.1% of the librarians they supervise are faculty
- 84.4% support librarians teaching in the disciplines
- 84.4% think that librarians teaching furthers the institution's mission; 8.9% think it does not; and 8.9% have no opinion
- 100% encourage librarians to become actively involved on campus

Directors were asked to choose why they supported librarians teaching–professional development; improvement of teaching skills; involvement in campus life; recognition as peer by teaching faculty. "Involvement in campus life" ranked highest, and "recognition as peer by teaching faculty" ranked a close second.

Several of the directors who responded were concerned about librarians teaching because they feared it would take time and energy away from library duties. One director said that librarians need to realize that they are librarians first and professors in some other discipline second.

Here are selected comments from the directors:

- I am concerned that librarians who also teach subject based courses will have a hard time fulfilling all their library duties without excessive stress.
- I would not want other librarians to have to pick up the slack.

- I can't imagine that faculty in biology would consider it part of their department's mission to teach a for credit course in English literature.
- I support [classroom teaching] for maintaining a high level of interest among my staff.
- I don't believe that faculty will recognize you as a peer just because you are teaching . . . the faculty are still an elite club which librarians are not recognized as being a part of . . .
- . . . librarians who refuse to be involved in campus activities and teaching, if qualified, are furthering a decline of the academic library as a vital part of the university campus.
- Either you are on the bus or off the bus. If librarians are faculty members then they must function as faculty members.
- I think it is essential that the library faculty teach in all areas.
- Librarians who have participated in teaching courses on campus have a broader understanding of the issues other faculty deal with on a regular basis.
- Teaching outside the library . . . provides the librarian with an opportunity to view library services and resources from the teacher's (and student's) perspective.
- While I support librarians teaching in other disciplines, I do not support them doing so on library time since they would be paid to teach a course in another discipline.
- I've taught . . . academic courses and found it very beneficial to my regular duties.
- Teaching faculty frequently know less about research in the general field in which they teach than do librarians.
- We do not have enough librarians to do the work needed to be done in our library; therefore, it would have a negative impact on library services for them to work less in their library jobs.

CONCLUSION

There are many benefits to the professor librarian model. Librarians get to know students and their needs in a way that is impossible in the traditional reference or library instruction model. Librarians with subject specialties get a chance to use their knowledge and pass it on. In the meantime, they are intellectually stimulated in a way that is not always possible in traditional library work. This also presents an opportunity for growth and renewal for librarians who have been performing the same duties for some time and need a change. They will reenter their library role with a new understanding of teaching and learning on campus and how they can be more engaged in that collective effort. They may even bring a new network of classroom faculty with whom they can work collaboratively to strengthen library instruction in the disciplines.

Librarians in classroom teaching roles gain a new understanding of the role of teaching faculty on campus. It's easy for us to grouse about the professor who rolls in at the last minute and wants something put on reserve for a class that starts in an hour; or the professor who turns in her materials request the week before classes begin; or the one who calls and wants a library instruction session for his class tomorrow morning. If you haven't been on the other side, you may think you know the pressures on teaching faculty, but you probably don't. In addition to time in class and time spent out of class working with individual students, I spent many evening hours placing materials on my Blackboard site, grading papers and tests, constructing fun and illustrative exercises, creating PowerPoint® presentations, and simply thinking of innovative ways to get the point across. Classroom faculty work with potentially hundreds of students each semester. Caring about each individual's growth and development takes time. Lots and lots of time.

Whether librarians teach outside the library or not, we need to learn to teach. We should know about learning theories, including multiple intelligences, and how to construct a class so that we reach learners of all abilities. Too many of us focus on what we think is important and not on what students need. We cram too much information into 50- or 80-minute sessions and don't allow time for students to reflect and retain the information. Library schools should teach courses in pedagogy and library directors should ensure that librarians have the training and support they need to be effective teachers.

I understand the concerns voiced by some of library directors. Indeed, I have performed the roles of head of reference, assistant director, and director at various institutions, and faced the necessity of staffing desks and getting work done when staffing was particularly tight. However, as a manager and librarian who keeps current with the literature on management and leadership, I favor coaching people to develop in ways that are congruent with the mission of the organization. Librarians who have the expertise, talent, and desire can serve the organization and enhance the reputation of the library at the same time. Teaching allows them to engage more profoundly in the teaching and learning community than their library role will ever allow them to.

SUGGESTIONS FOR FURTHER STUDY

While I was researching and writing this article, several questions came to mind and I offer them here as suggestions for further study:

- Does teaching in academic disciplines increase librarian's job satisfaction?
- When librarians teach in academic disciplines, does traditional library work suffer?
- Do students benefit when librarians teach English or history?
- What benefit, if any, accrues to the library when librarians teach in the disciplines?

The dearth of current articles in the reference list clearly indicates that more work can be done with the topic of librarians as teachers in academic disciplines. I hope that this contribution to the literature will spur interest and begin a conversation about the role of librarians as teachers.

REFERENCES

Borchuk, F. P. and Bergup, B. (1976). Opportunities and problems of college librarians involved in classroom teaching roles. ED 134 216.

Douglas, G. V. (1999). "Professor librarian: A model of the teaching librarian of the future. *Computers in Libraries 19* (10), 24-26+.

Hall, H. P. (1990). "Getting into the classroom in a non-bibliographic instruction way." In *The Librarian in the University: Essays on Membership in the Academic Community,* edited by H. P. Hall and C. Byrd. Metuchen, NJ: Scarecrow.

Leonard, W. P. (1989). More librarians should consider periodic classroom assignments. *Journal of Academic Librarianship 15,* 28+.

Sabol, C. (1977). Librarian in the Classroom. ED 150 985.

Yerburgh, M. R. (1979). The utilization of academic librarians as classroom teachers: Some brief observations. *Academe 65,* 441-443.

APPENDIX A

Librarians as Teachers in Academic Disciplines–A Survey

Dear Library Director:

I am writing an article on librarians as teachers for a forthcoming edition of *The Reference Librarian.* I invite you to participate by taking the following survey. Your anonymity is assured, unless you choose to share your name and institution with readers of the article.

Directions: Check the desired boxes and include your comments if so desired. Save the document to your desktop and return to me as an attachment.

Thank you.–Peggie Partello (contact info. below)

---

1. Are the librarians you supervise faculty?
   Yes ☐   No ☐

2. Do you support librarians teaching in the academic disciplines, i.e., outside the library? (Check one.)
   Yes ☐   No ☐

   2a. If yes, why? (Check all that apply.)
   Professional development ☐
   Improvement in teaching skills ☐
   Campus involvement ☐
   Recognition as peers by teaching faculty ☐

   Other (Please describe):

   2b. If no, why not? (Check all that apply.)
   Would take time away from library duties ☐
   Teaching in the disciplines should not be subsidized by library budget ☐
   Librarians don't have the appropriate discipline knowledge ☐
   Librarians don't have the appropriate teaching experience ☐
   Because the librarians I supervise are not faculty ☐

   Other (Please describe):

3. Do you think librarians teaching in the disciplines furthers the institution's mission? (Check one.)
   Yes ☐   No ☐   No Opinion ☐

4. Do you encourage librarians to be actively involved on campus? (Check one.)
   Yes ☐   No ☐

APPENDIX A (continued)

5. Do you have any comments? If so, include them here:

6. I agree to be identified by name and institution in the event the author includes some of my comments in the article.
    Yes ☐   No ☐

7. Would you agree to be interviewed? If so, please include your name, institutional affiliation, e-mail address, and telephone number.

Bonus Question: Do you support librarians engaging in professional development (other than attending conferences, workshops, etc.) in other locations in addition to the library?
                       Yes ☐   No ☐

Thank you for your participation.

Peggie Partello
Director, Curriculum Materials Library
Keene State College
229 Main St.
Keene, NH 03435-3201
ppartell@keene.edu
(603) 358-2729
fax: (603) 358-2745

APPENDIX B

Dear Librarian:

I am writing an article on librarians as teachers for a forthcoming edition of *The Reference Librarian*. I invite you to participate by taking the following survey. Your anonymity is assured, unless you choose to share your name and institution with readers of the article.

Directions: Check the desired boxes and include your comments if so desired. Save the document to your desktop and return to me as an attachment.

Thank you.–Peggie Partello (contact info. below)

---

1. Are you faculty?
   Yes ☐   No ☐

2. Do you teach library instruction?
   Yes ☐   No ☐

3. Do you have a subject specialty in addition to library and information science?
   Yes ☐   No ☐

4. Do you currently or have you in the past taught courses in academic disciplines, e.g., an English course?
   Yes ☐   No ☐

   4a. If yes, what do/did you like about the experience?
       Contributes to my professional development ☐
       Improves my teaching skills ☐
       Involves me in the life of the campus ☐
       Teaching faculty recognize me as a peer ☐
       Other (please describe):

   4b. If no, would you like the opportunity to teach a course in an academic discipline?
       Yes ☐   No ☐

5. Do you think librarians teaching in the disciplines furthers the institution's mission? (Check one.)
   Yes ☐   No ☐

6. I agree to be identified by name and institution in the event the author includes some of my comments in the article.
   Yes ☐   No ☐

7. Would you agree to be interviewed? If so, please include your name, institutional affiliation, e-mail address, and telephone number.

8. Do you have any comments? If so, include them here.

APPENDIX B (continued)

Bonus Question: Are you required to spend your work week in the library or can you
                     work in other locations? "Work" includes research, writing, and other
                     scholarship.
                     In library only ☐   May work in other locations ☐

Thank you for your participation.

Peggie Partello
Director, Curriculum Materials Library
Keene State College
229 Main St.
Keene, NH 03435-3201
ppartell@keene.edu
(603) 358-2729
fax: (603) 358-2745

Faculty-Librarian Collaboration to Teach Research Skills: Electronic Symbiosis

Navaz P. Bhavnagri
Veronica Bielat

SUMMARY. This article discusses faculty-librarian collaboration to integrate technology in a course that focuses on teaching empirical research methodologies and library research skills to elementary and early childhood education graduate students. Vygotsky's theory, standards in teacher education, and information literacy standards form the conceptual framework that supports this collaboration. The purpose and procedures of this collaboration, as well as student, faculty, and librarian outcomes, are discussed. This present collaboration on bibliographic instruction and the use of Blackboard courseware is framed within the context of past history of collaboration and future plans to expand this collaboration. *[Article copies available for a fee from The Haworth Document Delivery Service: 1-800-HAWORTH. E-mail address: <docdelivery@haworthpress.com> Website: <http://www.HaworthPress.com> © 2005 by The Haworth Press, Inc. All rights reserved.]*

Navaz P. Bhavnagri (E-mail: nbhavna@wayne.edu) is Associate Professor, Early Childhood Education, and Veronica Bielat (E-mail: vbielat@wayne.edu) is Information Services Librarian and Liaison, both at the College of Education, Wayne State University, Detroit, MI 48202.

[Haworth co-indexing entry note]: "Faculty-Librarian Collaboration to Teach Research Skills: Electronic Symbiosis." Bhavnagri, Navaz P., and Veronica Bielat. Co-published simultaneously in *The Reference Librarian* (The Haworth Information Press, an imprint of The Haworth Press, Inc.) No. 89/90, 2005, pp. 121-138; and: *Relationships Between Teaching Faculty and Teaching Librarians* (ed: Susan B. Kraat) The Haworth Information Press, an imprint of The Haworth Press, Inc., 2005, pp. 121-138. Single or multiple copies of this article are available for a fee from The Haworth Document Delivery Service [1-800-HAWORTH, 9:00 a.m. - 5:00 p.m. (EST). E-mail address: docdelivery@haworthpress.com].

http://www.haworthpress.com/web/REF
© 2005 by The Haworth Press, Inc. All rights reserved.
Digital Object Identifier: 10.1300/J120v43n89_09

KEYWORDS. Academic libraries, bibliographic instruction, collaboration, courseware, critical thinking, education students, faculty-librarian relationship, information literacy, library research, technology

Nesbitt states, "Preparing future teachers to meet information technology and research challenges requires the collaborative development of instructional strategies by both education faculty and academic librarians" (5). This article documents the collaboration between an education faculty member and academic librarian in providing instructional strategies on information technology and research skills for future and current teachers. This faculty-librarian electronic symbiosis took place in a course that focuses on research methodologies, offered to elementary and early childhood education master's level students in Wayne State University's (WSU) College of Education. One of the course objectives is for students to learn to access, analyze and synthesize information using library resources. Therefore, a library instruction session has always been included at the beginning of this course.

CONCEPTUAL FRAMEWORK FOR COLLABORATION

Mattessich and Monsey (Cook 23) define collaboration as a mutually beneficial undertaking to achieve common goals, supported by a well-designed structure. Our "common goal" is to have students achieve the course objectives stated above. The foundation of our "well designed collaborative structure" is first based on Vygotsky's conceptual framework of "scaffolding" and "zone of proximal development."

In Berk and Winsler (26-27, 171) and Bodrova and Leong (42-43, 162), scaffolding is described as a process by which individuals gradually learn with support, guidance, and direction from experts (such as adults or peers) until they finally work independently. In this collaborative effort, the librarian acts as expert, scaffolding the faculty member's skills in technology; the faculty member as an expert, scaffolding the librarian's knowledge of research and teaching pedagogy; and the faculty member and librarian (as peers) collaborating to scaffold students' research methods, knowledge and skills. Finally, it is our contention that in addition to our actions as experts in the scaffolding process, technology can scaffold student learning because it is an expert educational tool that provides support and direction students need to learn, especially when the human expert (e.g., faculty or librarian) is not available to provide immediate assistance.

The zone of proximal development (ZPD) is a dynamic region between where an individual can accomplish independently to where a person can develop, learn and accomplish with assistance from a competent person (e.g., adult or peer) (Berk and Winsler 24-26 and Bodrova and Leong 34-47). This zone is an elastic area of development, which varies with the individual. The lower limit of ZPD demonstrates development that is achievable without intervention from a competent person or "expert," while the upper limit of ZPD demonstrates development of the student or "novice" with assisted performance (Wink and Putney 86). According to Vygotsky, when an expert (such as the faculty member or librarian) scaffolds a novice (such as the student) to the upper limit of ZPD, then it is a movement towards higher learning processes. Thus the new concepts which were first understood only within an inter-personal relationship between the expert and novice (i.e., lower ZPD) are finally becoming internalized and intra-personal, and the learner has now reached the level where they can work independently (i.e., upper ZPD).

Second, our collaborative structure is based on the WSU College of Education Conceptual Framework, guided by The National Council for Accreditation of Teacher Education (NCATE) Accreditation of Schools, Colleges, and Departments of Education professional standards (2002). The WSU Conceptual Framework states that it is a desirable outcome when "[the student] uses technology as an integral part of one's teaching and learning and is both a learner and a model of the use of technology in educational settings" (COE WSU).

Third, our collaborative structure is based on The American College and Research Library's (ACRL) Information Literacy Competency Standards for Higher Education. For this collaboration, we specifically focused on the ACRL Standard Two, namely the abilities to access needed information effectively and efficiently; Standard Three, namely the ability to critically evaluate information and sources and incorporate them into the student's knowledge base; and Standard Four, namely the ability to use information effectively to accomplish a specific purpose. These three standards parallel the intended outcomes stated in the course syllabus.

PAST:
LIBRARIAN-FACULTY COLLABORATION
AND TECHNOLOGY

History of Collaboration

The following narrative discusses the changes in the library instruction process with the advent of technology, resulting in significant shifts in student participation and faculty-librarian collaboration. A decade ago, computers were not used in the library instruction for this course, since they were available only in public areas of the main floor of the library. Furthermore, there were few electronic databases available, and the librarians always mediated the students' searches. The librarian at that time provided printed handouts describing the complex computer search processes and lectured students on the mechanics of searching the ERIC database. The faculty member recollects that the students did not fully comprehend, retain or implement much of the information. Perhaps this was partly due to the method of delivery, and partly due to the students' unfamiliarity with computers.

As integration of technology into the library advanced, the librarian would then roll a computer into the classroom for the instruction session. Students would receive a lecture on search strategies, supplemented with handouts. The class would then gather around the single computer to view an active search. The students were excited, because they were now able to see a demonstration of a computer search by the librarian in real-time.

The faculty member was silent during these earlier phases of technology integration into the bibliographic instruction session. First, she was quiet because she viewed this to be the "librarian's turf," area of expertise, and to show respect to the librarian during her delivery. Second, she herself had limited computer skills. Third, there were no individual student computer stations for the faculty member to assist the librarian in supervising the students. Thus the collaboration between the faculty member and the librarian during instruction was minimal to non-existent.

The installation of computer labs in the library drastically shifted the teaching-learning process. Now the students in this course could simultaneously execute searches along with the librarian's demonstration. However, the bibliographic instruction session was still scripted. Namely, the students executed specific searches as prescribed by the librarian on a predetermined topic, but the students in class did not apply these generic scripted strategies to their own specific research question. Despite it, the students were still elated because they could now participate in a hands-on activity using individual computers. The faculty member also began to actively collaborate in this teaching process, because for the first time there were multiple students' computer stations for her to monitor. The librarian and the faculty member thus began to communicate with each other about students' progress and problems.

Today, bibliographic instruction sessions take place in computer labs with interactive Smartboards, high-speed Internet networks and individual student workstations. The librarian now increasingly addresses the students individually by circulating among them for the following reasons. First, unlike before, the Smartboard allows her to move away from her demonstration workstation. Second, the students require even more individual attention now than before, given that the number of electronic resources available has increased substantially. Third, even though students today have more advanced computer skills than a decade ago, there is still a wide variation in their abilities, thus requiring individual attention.

The faculty member now collaborates with the librarian by being actively engaged in providing this well needed individualized guidance. Since the faculty member's knowledge and skills in technology have also increased over time, she is more confident to provide the necessary direct instruction and individualized supervision. Given the volume of library resources available and the complexity of the research process, bibliographic instruction has been expanded from a single session at the beginning of this fifteen-week course into two consecutive sessions. As a result, there is now time in class for students to apply the generic search strategies to their specific research questions, which students find very reassuring. The faculty member additionally collaborates with the librarian by providing her feedback on students' successes and failures in applying the library instruction in subsequent weeks. To summarize, growth in collaboration is due to an increase in technology, faculty member's expertise and her active engagement in instruction.

PRESENT:
LIBRARIAN-FACULTY COLLABORATION
AND TECHNOLOGY

The collaborative effort in providing bibliographic instruction, and the development of a Blackboard course site, is described here within the Vygotskian framework. The following narrative is based on the faculty member's journal of students' reactions to technology and her feedback; the librarian's recorded field notes on technological assistance to students and the faculty member; students' communications on Blackboard's discussion boards; and students' responses to an online survey, which was created and administered by the librarian and the faculty member. The students' responses to the survey provide anecdotal evidence of shifts in their ZPD. However, these responses have not been subjected to statistical scrutiny. This entire section is written from an outsider's perspective. First, we review the purpose for scaffolding. Next, we discuss the procedure for this collaborative process. Last, we examine the upper limit of librarian, faculty member and students' ZPD as outcomes of this collaboration.

Bibliographic Instruction

Purpose: Scaffolding

The bibliographic instruction scaffolded the students to reach several purposes.

Understand their electronic identity. According to Vygotsky, for novices to reach their upper ZPD, they often need experts scaffolding them verbally and experts performing actions on cultural tools, such as computers. Thus the librarian, who was the expert, verbally explained to the students, who were novices, the purpose and value of their electronic user ID and password identification. She further scaffolded them by her actions on the computer, when she demonstrated to them how to log on.

Results from the post-bibliographic instruction online survey indicated that more than 17% of the respondents did not even know their user ID, which is their "key" to electronic library and campus resources. Without this knowledge, these students would not be able to perform a myriad of tasks, e.g., access the electronic resources, the Blackboard courseware or their grades, or register for classes. Vygotsky states that conceptual understanding is only purposeful and valuable when it arises to answer a real problem within an actual social context (Harvey and Charnitski 152).

Develop a mental model of electronic library resources. The electronic library resources do not offer the same obvious visual tools and signs for structuring information that are readily apparent in paper-based indexes and card catalogs. Furthermore, most electronic databases are unique commercial products; therefore, the organization and display of information can be very different between products, which further confounds the students' mental models of electronic data.

Students typically come to this course with a mental model of print media, or an inflexible and limited model of electronic media, all of which need "reshaping." Brandt says, "in order to teach effectively, librarians must understand users' mental models" (42). We further add, that the librarian must not simply "understand users' mental models" but also scaffold the students to revise their earlier mental model on information processing, to move them to the upper limit of their ZPD, for example, scaffolding students to develop mental models of a database, record fields and how the computer executes the search, in order to develop an effective search strategy. Thus, a mental model "is a complicated set of knowledge and beliefs which is used both as a source of referent understanding and as a tool for problem solving" (Brandt 42), which needs scaffolding by an expert such as a librarian.

Scaffold critical thinking skills. Murray, McKee and Hammons (107, 108) state that many graduate College of Education students are not competent in fully utilizing technology and doing independent library research for producing high quality research papers, despite living in an "information age." Our students in the master's program at Wayne State University also need to develop competency in producing high quality research papers, by developing critical thinking skills. These skills are at their lower ZPD and need scaffolding. According to Bodi, Ruggiero's third stage in teaching of critical thinking, namely the "investigation stage," is applicable to bibliographic instruction (70-71). Therefore, our students were first taught how to critically examine and investigate multiple sources in order to determine what kinds of sources would yield the most useful and relevant information. Both the librarian and the faculty member collaboratively introduced these discerning skills during the bibliographic instruction sessions, when the librarian assumed the role of expert.

During the semester, the role of expert was transferred to the faculty member, who actively taught these critical thinking skills throughout the semester. She used multiple scaffolding strategies such as role modeling, teaching the use of library resources to narrow their dependent and independent variables, teaching how to critique published research articles, and drafts of their research questions and hypothesis. Thus the students were scaffolded to develop higher-level skills in searching, identification and evaluation of research materials.

Procedure: Collaborative Process

The faculty member was present at both bibliographic instruction sessions. During these two instruction sessions, librarian, faculty member and students maintained an ongoing dialogue about search strategy, resource appropriateness, and scholarly research. For example, the librarian used both live search and a PowerPoint® presentation when introducing ERIC. Concurrently, the faculty member collaborated with the librarian by redefining library terminology, by verbally emphasizing resources and search methodology suggested by the librarian, and finally by reiterating important concepts stated by the librarian. Through this type of "verbal underlining" the faculty member communicated to the students that the librarian's messages had an "added value," a deeper meaning, and were relevant and applicable to the forthcoming course assignments. The librarian and faculty member thus equally participated in the delivery of information to develop information literacy skills in students. According to Vygotsky, knowledge was being co-constructed (developing joint knowledge by dialogue). Although the starting point and delivery of information may have differed, the information communication goals for both the faculty member and librarian were the same. Vygotsky calls this inter-subjectivity. The librarian and faculty member had voices in this communication process, during which "each communicant recognizes the echo of the original text [the information message] in the other's speech" (Kozulin 186).

Arp and Wilson (27) have developed structures of library instruction, identifying varying typologies of cooperation between the librarian and others. One of their structures is conceived as "Course Integrated Instruction." In this structure the bibliographic instruction becomes an integral part of the course because the "integration [of instruction] is usually achieved by discussion between faculty and librarians at the time the course is designed." It is this structure that best resembles our collaborative process. The faculty member's discussions with the librarian began in earnest when this graduate course was being redesigned to integrate computer technologies.

Outcomes: Upper ZPD

The electronic searches scaffolded students, the faculty member, and the librarian to reach higher mental processes at the upper limit of ZPD.

Student. The goal of the bibliographic instruction sessions was to take the students from a lower level ZPD to an upper level ZPD, by attaining information literacy outcomes as described in the ACRL guidelines. When surveyed on skill self-assessment, 100% of the students reported their library search skills were better than when they had begun the class. In addition, 60% of the students reported that using the library resources facilitated their learning of research methods and concepts. The post-class survey dramatically provides a visual sense of their achievement, indicating their upper level of ZPD. For example, knowledge without assistance is reported in Figure 1. Knowledge with assistance is reported in Figure 2. The students believe that their level of expertise has increased after scaffolding.

Faculty. This collaboration with the librarian enhanced the faculty member's awareness of new resources and strategies that are useful in personal research, thus moving her to the upper level of her ZPD. Frequent social discourse about these searches with the librarian followed by self-reflection has increasingly expanded her zone, promoted interpersonal to intra-personal development, and further convinced her of the value of dialectic materialism. Her developmental shifts are similar to what Torres reported about teacher-researchers (2).

Librarian. This collaboration broadened the librarian's understanding of the faculty member's expectations of student outcomes on library assignments. This insight led to the development of handouts and a PowerPoint® presentation on search strategies that have been effectively applied in bibliographic instruction for this course and other education courses.

Blackboard

Purpose: Scaffolding

Blackboard was employed by the faculty member in this course as a mediating strategy to scaffold students.

Self-instruction. The information available on Blackboard was to scaffold their learning at their own pace. Examples of self-instructional electronic scaffolds were: text chapter study guides, written instructions for each assignment, rubrics for self-evaluation, examples of previous students' exemplary assignments, and PowerPoint® presentations supporting each week's class content.

FIGURE 1. Student Survey Responses on ERIC Expertise Showing Lower Limit ZPD

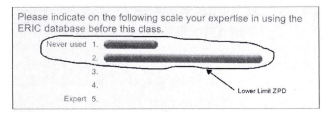

FIGURE 2. Student Survey Responses on ERIC Expertise Showing Upper Limit ZPD

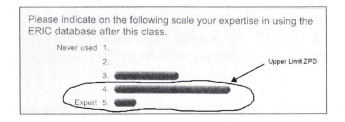

Promote peer teaching, communication and support. Student discussion boards were developed in Blackboard as communication tools. First, a class-wide discussion board was provided as a forum for peer teaching where students could suggest strategies on how to further refine their research questions and hypothesis. Second, discussion boards for group presentations on research methods were available to students, as a convenient 24/7 alternative to face-to-face and telephone communications. For example: these were designed to save on phone bills, campus parking costs, travel time for face-to face meetings, and alleviate the difficulty of finding a common time to meet on campus. Finally, a discussion board was specifically designed to support and encourage students to ventilate their affect when learning about technology, because brain research clearly shows that affect can mediate cognition (Bergen and Cogcia).

Procedure: Collaborative Process

The development and maintenance of the Blackboard course site was the faculty member's responsibility. The librarian provided support to the faculty member in maintaining the course site throughout the semester, by constantly communicating via e-mail, face-to-face and telephone conferencing, especially on Friday afternoons. The faculty member would share her vision and concept of what she would like in Blackboard and the librarian would respond, based on her technical expertise. A discussion would then follow as to other possibilities or pursuing the vision as stated.

Second, this collaborative effort on Blackboard was effective only because the faculty member and the librarian invested enormous amounts of time, energy and effort, which resulted in successes, but also many false starts of undoing and redoing the postings to Blackboard. At other times, they had to call on other experts, such as faculty and staff of curriculum and technology, to scaffold them in the knowledge and skills required to achieve their stated goal. Thus, this kind of true collaborative effort involves juggling one's ongoing myriad of responsibilities, being disciplined, balancing the workload, and creating a flexible schedule (Winner 27-28). Regardless of how onerous a task it may seem, multiple scholars (e.g., Cook 25, Cardwell 257, Zhang 141) have reiterated that faculty-librarian collaboration is a worthwhile endeavor because it significantly contributes to the librarian's professional development.

Third, this collaboration on the development of the Blackboard course site was a symbiotic relationship because the faculty member and the librarian had complimentary expertise. The faculty member had content knowledge of information, and the librarian had the necessary technological skills. For example, the faculty member had published in electronic journals but did not know how to link her articles to the Blackboard site. This was made possible by the librarian's expertise. The librarian also taught the faculty member how to make the documents available in multiple formats to enhance and simplify student access. The faculty member and the librarian continued to share different skills and knowledge as the collaboration progressed.

Fourth, the faculty member and librarian collaborated to teach students how to access the Blackboard course site. Even though over 80% of students knew their WSU access ID at the beginning of the class, many of them had difficulty logging on to Blackboard, and accessing and downloading course materials. While the faculty member gave a tour of the Blackboard site to the entire class, the librarian provided individual assistance to students experiencing difficulty in accessing the courseware. This strategy of the group touring the courseware along with individualized support from the librarian is imperative, as it is insufficient to merely announce to students that there is a Blackboard site available for the course and to expect them to fully utilize it as a scaffolding tool. Just as the syllabus needs reviewing in detail at the beginning of a course, so does the Blackboard course site.

Outcomes: Upper ZPD

The use of Blackboard scaffolded the students, the faculty member, and the librarian to reach higher mental processes at the upper limit of ZPD.

Student. First, access to the materials on Blackboard was self-instructional to move to the upper limit of their ZPD. Kuhlthau's stage model has identified that students feel apprehension, uncertainty, confusion and anxiety when tackling research assignments (237-240). These negative affects impede student progress in reaching their upper limit of ZPD. Easy access to materials on Blackboard counteracted this phenomenon. Using the courseware, the faculty member mounted several sample assignments for student reference. As a result, the faculty member observed that students demonstrated more confidence by submitting more criticality in their reviews of research literature. They did not repeatedly ask for clarification of assignment details, as students have typically done in the past, thus demonstrating less anxiety about their performance. Finally, the availability of a textbook study guide on Blackboard enhanced student comprehension.

Second, it was most effective in promoting communication and support as evidenced by survey responses (see Figure 3–Student Responses to Survey Questions 11 and 12), but less so in peer teaching. Students used the Blackboard discussion boards early in the semester to successfully communicate their research question and hypothesis. However, students did not take the risk of teaching by improving on their peer's hypothesis. By the end of the semester, a few students had moved to an upper level of their ZPD in peer teaching by suggesting improvements to their peers' research question and/or hypothesis. The discussion boards served the overall purpose of promoting peer communication. Through their design, and by being based on the Vygotskian premise, they advanced collective knowledge, communication and support, which in turn led to individuals' gaining knowledge and confidence, and reducing students' uncertainty and anxiousness (Hung and Nichani 5).

A special discussion board was designed for students' emotional catharsis and for them to vent the challenges they faced in using the technology. We found that it actually provided a forum beyond catharsis, to

FIGURE 3. Student Responses to Survey Questions 11 and 12

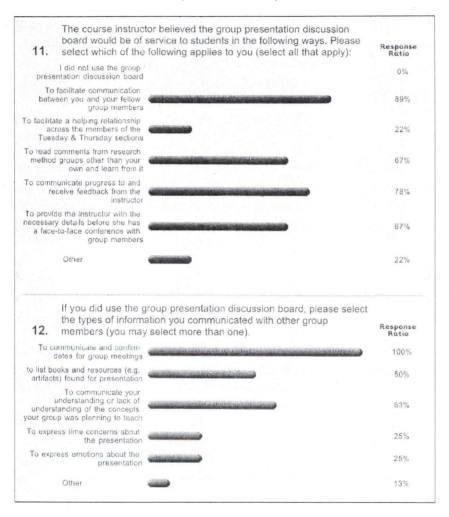

resolution of the problems that confronted them. Students who were "experts" in technology communicated to "novices" the relevant strategies regarding resolving technology problems, thus moving the "novices" to the upper limit of their ZPD. Providing this avenue for self-expression of emotions appeared to reduce their overall frustration over technology, and freed them to focus on higher cognitive processing.

Faculty. First, Blackboard scaffolded the faculty member to know students as individuals and build her relationship with them, especially those students who typically did not talk in class but felt comfortable communicating with her via Blackboard. Additionally, by reading their communications to each other, she knew their concerns and could steadily monitor individual progress.

Second, Blackboard scaffolded the faculty member to teach and monitor students' group presentations. For example: she came to know of each individual member's contribution to the group; she monitored their process of decision-making by complimenting and redirecting them with specific suggestions; and she was better prepared when the students shared their plans about their group presentations, resulting in shorter conferences. The discussion boards in Blackboard made the faculty member more available between class sessions. This availability, in turn, increased her opportunities to be more effective in relationship building, teaching, and monitoring, thus moving her to the upper limit of her ZPD.

Librarian. The development of the Blackboard course site scaffolded the librarian by expanding her knowledge of course content, particularly the six research methods. The librarian, by working with the faculty member, better understood how to incorporate an electronic component, such as Blackboard, into teaching pedagogy. Finally, the librarian was regularly able to gain knowledge about students' abilities and difficulties, and discover areas in the delivery of library instruction that needed revision. This was a direct result of her access to the student discussion boards.

FUTURE:
LIBRARIAN-FACULTY COLLABORATION
AND TECHNOLOGY

In this section we discuss plans for future collaborations in providing bibliographic instruction and further enhancing the Blackboard course site.

Bibliographic Instruction

Develop Instructional and Evaluative Materials

We plan to design two instructional materials. First, we will develop a PowerPoint® presentation on critical thinking skills in evaluating library sources. This presentation will contain samples of available electronic documents and journals collaboratively selected by the librarian and the faculty member. Students will be able to immediately connect their new evaluative skills with appropriate examples. This co-teaching is designed on Bodi's recommendations (1992, 72) that students' critical thinking skills for evaluating sources can be best enhanced when librarians and faculty are instructing collaboratively and in unison.

Second, we plan to develop an interactive instructional electronic worksheet where students systematically record appropriate database search strategies. The purpose of this worksheet is for students to self-evaluate their ability to apply what is taught in class; and for us to find out which specific strategies are unclear to them, so that we may revisit them in the next session. The ACRL's Education and Behavioral Sciences Section Bibliographic Instruction for Educators Committee recommended that such a worksheet with instructions for ERIC and blanks for strategy formulation would be a desirable tool for teaching information retrieval and evaluation skills (ACRL 588).

We also plan to design two sets of evaluative materials. The first is a revision of the rubric used to evaluate students' electronic search journals. The faculty member unilaterally designed the current rubric but the future rubric will be collaboratively constructed. Furthermore, the revised rubric will be based on information literacy standards and the conceptual framework of the WSU College of Education, which addresses the NCATE standards. Second, we will develop and administer a quiz through Blackboard after the bibliographic instruction sessions. This quiz will be designed on Cudiner and Harmon's (1) suggestions for promoting active learning in students; and on Brandt's recommendation to identify learners' existing mental models of information organization and retrieval in order to provide a matching teaching strategy for information literacy.

Role Meshing

Cardwell (254, 255) advises that to truly facilitate student learning, the librarian must also act as an instructor. We believe that for this course, the faculty member must also act as a reference librarian. Therefore, in the future, the faculty member will be available in the library during her office hours in the weeks immediately following the bibliographic instruction sessions, to guide students with their library research. In the future, the librarian will be an instructor electronically. This will be accomplished through the development of a separate librarian discussion board in Blackboard. This discussion board will thus send an explicit message to the students that the librarian is an instructor who is accessible throughout the semester, and her availability is not limited to the two bibliographic instruction sessions.

Blackboard

Photographic Instruction

Most students enrolled in this course are newly admitted into the master's program and are therefore unfamiliar with the vast library resources available. Hence, we plan to mount floor maps in Blackboard of various locations in the library with digital photographs of: circulation, reference and reserved material desks; separate stacks for journals and books; area for displaying the recent journals; inter-library loan services; microfiche research area, and main floor computer area. We anticipate that this self-instructive electronic walking tour of the library will help students feel less overwhelmed when they have to go to the library to access materials.

Video Instruction

We will upload video clips demonstrating students' exemplary presentations on research methods, for example: role-playing and conducting interviews and focus groups; coding video taped observations; and analyzing artifacts and documents for case studies, and ethnographic and historical research. These videos will be enhanced by written products related to these clips such as: interview protocol, focus group discussion guide, observation coding system, matrix for analyzing the artifacts for a case study, a webbing chart indicating triangulation of data in ethnography, and a rubric for historical criticism of documents. There are two purposes for these exhibits: first, to facilitate teaching students to visualize how to plan, conduct and evaluate their constructivist group presentations, and second, for the faculty member to explain the rubric used for evaluating their group presentations.

CONCLUSION

Our narrative has described how our collaborative effort evolved, and we expect our collaboration to continue from an interpersonal to synergetic level (Raspa and Ward). According to Raspa and Ward, the interpersonal level of a collaboration is where "the partners begin to explore both personal and interdisciplinary areas of interest, and may undertake small projects" (12). We began this collaboration by exploring our "personal and interdisciplinary areas of interest" and undertook bibliographic instruction and integration of Blackboard as our "small project" for a course focusing on research methods.

We believe we have moved into the beginnings of the synergetic level, which means "the boundaries separating the disciplines begin to blur" (Raspa and Ward 13). Our role boundaries as librarian and faculty have already been blurred as documented in our present collaboration, and the process of writing this article in a collaborative manner has further advanced us to a synergetic level. Our future plans documented in this article further blurs our roles, resulting in a seamless delivery of course content to our students. Our vision is of continuous long-term collaboration that sustains this high level of synergy, which will result in even more effective outcomes benefiting all learners–faculty, librarians and students.

REFERENCES

Arp, Lori, and Lizabeth A. Wilson. "Structures of Bibliographic Instruction Programs: A Continuum for Planning." *Reference Librarian* 24 (1989): 25-34.

Association of College & Research Libraries. Education and Behavioral Sciences Section. Bibliographic Instruction for Educators Committee (1991-1992). "Information retrieval and evaluation skills for education students." *C&RL News* 9 (1992): 583-588.

Association of College & Research Libraries. *Information Literacy Competency Standards for Higher Education: Standards, Performance Indicators, and Outcomes.* Chicago: ACRL, 2000. 4 March 2003 <http://www.ala.org/acrl/ilstandardlo.html>.

Bergen, Doris and Juliet Coscia. *Brain Research and Childhood Education: Implications for Education.* Olney MD: ACEI, 2001.

Berk, Laura E., and Adam Winsler. *Scaffolding Children's Learning: Vygotsky and Early Childhood Education.* NAEYC Research into Practice Ser. 7. Washington: NAEYC, 1995.

Bodi, Sonia. "Collaborating with Faculty in Teaching Critical Thinking: The Role of Librarians." *Research Strategies* 102 (1992): 69-76.

Bodrova, Elena, and Deborah J. Leong. *Tools of the Mind: The Vygotskian Approach to Early Childhood Education.* Englewood Cliffs: Prentice-Hall, 1996.

Brandt, D. Scott. "Reference, Mental Models and Teaching Technology." *The Reference Librarian* 74 (2001): 37-47.

Cardwell, Catherine. "Faculty: An Essential Resource for Reference Librarians. At Bowling Green State University." *The Reference Librarian* 73 (2001): 253-63.

College of Education, Wayne State University. *Conceptual Framework Report.* Detroit: COE WSU. 5 April 2003. <http://www.coe.wayne.edu/conceptual_ framework.htm>.

Cook, Doug. "Creating Connections: A Review of the Literature." *The Collaborative Imperative: Librarians and Faculty Working Together in the Information Universe.* Ed. Richard Raspa and Dane Ward. Chicago: ACRL, 2000. 19-38.

Cudiner, Shelley, and Oskar R. Harmon. "An Active Learning Approach to Teaching Effective Online Search Strategies: A Librarian/Faculty Collaboration." *T.H.E. Journal* 28.5 (2000): 52-7.

Harvey, Francis A. and Christina Wodell Charnitski. "Improving Mathematics Instruction Using Technology: A Vygotskian Perspective." ERIC, 1998. ED 423 837.

Hung, David Wei Loong and Maish Nichani. "Bringing Communities of Practice into Schools: Implications for Instructional Technologies from Vygotskian Perspectives." *International Journal of Instructional Media* 29 (2002): 171-183.

Kozulin, Alex. *Vygotsky's Psychology: A Biography of Ideas.* New York: Harvester Wheatsheaf, 1990.

Kuhlthau, Carol C. "Developing a mental model of the library search process: Cognitive and affective aspects." RQ 28 (1988). 232-242.

Murray, Jr., John W., Elizabeth Chadbourn McKee and James O. Hammons. "Faculty and Librarian Collaboration: The Road to Information Literacy for Graduate Students." *Journal on Excellence in College Teaching* 8 (1997): 107-121.

National Council for Accreditation of Teacher Education. *Professional Standards for the Accreditation of Schools, Colleges, and Departments of Education.* Washington: NCATE, 2002. 4 March 2003 <http://www.ncate.org/2000/unit_stnds_ 2002.pdf>.

Nesbitt, Renee. "Faculty-Librarian Partnerships." *Education Libraries* 21 (1997): 5-11.

Raspa, Richard, and Dane Ward. "Listening for Collaboration: Faculty and Librarians Working Together." *The Collaborative Imperative: Librarians and Faculty Working Together in the Information Universe.* Ed. Richard Raspa and Dane Ward. Chicago: ACRL, 2000. 1-18.

Torres, Myriam N. "Teacher-Researchers in the 'Zone of Proximal Development': Insights for Teacher Education." ERIC, 1996. ED 410 189.

Vygotsky, Lev Semenovich. *Thought and Language.* Trans. Eugenia Hanfmann and Gertrude Vakar. Cambridge: MIT P, 1962.

Wink, Joan, and LeAnn Putney. *A Vision of Vygotsky.* Boston: Allyn and Bacon, 2002.

Winner, Marian C. "Librarians as Partners in the Classroom: An Increasing Imperative." *Reference Services Review* 26 (1998): 25-30.

Zhang, Wenxian. "Building Partnerships in Liberal Arts Education: Library Team Teaching." *Reference Services Review* 29 (2001): 141-149.

An Ethnographic Study of Attitudes Influencing Faculty Collaboration in Library Instruction

Kate Manuel
Susan E. Beck
Molly Molloy

SUMMARY. Numerous surveys over the years have found that faculty value librarians more for their reference work, often described as "service," than for their contributions to teaching; that 55-85 percent of faculty report using no LI with their classes; and that faculty have various reasons for not using librarian-provided instruction. This study differs from its predecessors by focusing specifically upon faculty who use LI heavily with their courses and interviewing them about why they use LI and what they value about it. Understanding these faculty members' values regard-

Kate Manuel (E-mail: kmanuel@lib.nmsu.edu) is Instruction Coordinator, Susan E. Beck (E-mail:susabeck@lib.nmsu.edu) is Head, Reference and Research Services, and Molly Molloy (E-mail: mmolloy@lib.nmsu.edu) is Reference Librarian and Latin American Bibliographer, all at New Mexico State University Library, MSC 4375, New Mexico State University, P.O. Box 30006, Las Cruces, NM 88003-8006.

The authors would like to thank Irene Shown, Reference Assistant, for her assistance in transcribing and organizing the transcriptions of the interviews discussed in this paper.

[Haworth co-indexing entry note]: "An Ethnographic Study of Attitudes Influencing Faculty Collaboration in Library Instruction." Manuel, Kate, Susan E. Beck, and Molly Molloy. Co-published simultaneously in *The Reference Librarian* (The Haworth Information Press, an imprint of The Haworth Press, Inc.) No. 89/90, 2005, pp. 139-161; and: *Relationships Between Teaching Faculty and Teaching Librarians* (ed: Susan B. Kraat) The Haworth Information Press, an imprint of The Haworth Press, Inc., 2005, pp. 139-161. Single or multiple copies of this article are available for a fee from The Haworth Document Delivery Service [1-800-HAWORTH, 9:00 a.m. - 5:00 p.m. (EST). E-mail address: docdelivery@haworthpress.com].

http://www.haworthpress.com/web/REF
Digital Object Identifier: 10.1300/J120v43n89_10

ing LI, as expressed in their own words, can assist librarians in promoting course-integrated instruction. *[Article copies available for a fee from The Haworth Document Delivery Service: 1-800-HAWORTH. E-mail address: <docdelivery@haworthpress.com> Website: <http://www.HaworthPress.com>*

KEYWORDS. Library instruction, librarian-faculty collaboration, faculty culture

INTRODUCTION

Librarians' continuing interest in faculty attitudes toward librarians and library instruction (LI) is understandable given that their opportunities for educating students are largely shaped by faculty attitudes, especially by faculty commitment to students' conducting library or information research and by their receptiveness to course-integrated LI. As Knapp emphasized: "Neither subject field, nor teaching method, nor kind of assignment, nor quality of student in a class is of crucial importance in determining whether or not a given course will be dependent on the library. The only decisive factor seemed to be–and this is a subjective judgment–the instructor's attitude. Where the instructor expected and planned for student use, it occurred. Where he did not, it did not occur" (1958, 829).[1] Prior studies have thus concentrated upon faculty's general views of librarians as fellow participants in higher education, faculty's use of and attitudes toward library research assignments and LI, and faculty's rationales for *not* availing themselves of librarian-provided instruction.

Surveys of academic faculty often corroborate librarians' fears that teaching faculty view them as, at best, bit players in the academic enterprise. Ivey found that "even when librarians have faculty status, teaching faculty do not consider them their academic equals" (1994, 79).[2] Faculty more often value librarians for work at the reference desk, often described as "service," than for teaching (Ivey 1994, 70 & 81).[3] Most faculty rated librarians' roles in teaching information skills as moderate to low, in marked contrast to the high ranking that they give to the role of library research in students' education. Forty-two percent of respondents in one study thus felt that librarians had "only 'some' involvement in the educational process" (Divay, Ducas & Michaud-Oystryk 1987, 31),[4] yet, another study found that "[f]aculty from all departments overwhelmingly agreed that library research is important in their fields"

(Cannon 1994, 526).[5] In keeping with the finding that faculty value the educational potential of libraries generally but not the educational role of librarians in particular, few faculty members report making use of librarian-provided instruction with their classes. Various studies report that 55 to 85 percent of faculty *do not* use librarian-provided instruction (Divay, Ducas & Michaud-Oystryk 1987; Ducas and Michaud-Oystryk 2003; Feldman & Sciammarella 2000; Gonzales 2001; Haws, Peterson & Shonrock 1989; Leckie & Fullerton 1999; Maynard 1990; Sellen & Jirouch 1984; Thomas 1994).[6]

Faculty members express numerous reasons for not using LI with their courses. Some report that they are teaching courses that do not involve library research (Leckie & Fullerton, 1999, 17).[7] Others note that it is difficult to fit LI into their courses, a sentiment seemingly becoming more pervasive among faculty (Thomas 1994, 213).[8] Librarians' being insufficiently knowledgeable about the discipline to provide LI is a factor cited by some faculty members, often those in the sciences (Ducas & Michaud-Oystryk 2003, 58).[9] Sizable numbers of faculty on some campuses reported not knowing that LI was an option (Cannon 1994, 531).[10] Some faculty feel that LI is unnecessary because students *should know* how to do research, having learned this either from other, typically general education, courses (Lubans 1980) [11] or by "osmosis" (Cannon 1994, 528). Others believe students *should* learn library and information research skills on their own (Gonzales 2001, 196),[12] as faculty have (Thomas 1994, 213).[13] Some faculty prefer to do their own LI (Cannon 1994, 531; Gonzales 2001, 198). Yet others would rather their students ask them, or a librarian, for assistance as needed (Feldman & Sciammarella 2000, 494; Thomas 1994, 216). Dissatisfaction with LI is another factor in some faculty members' decisions not to use it (Feldman & Sciammarella 2000, 494; Sinn 2000, 24). Finally, some report difficulties in scheduling LI with the library (Cannon 1994, 531).

The current study builds upon its predecessors, while differing from them in several ways. Much prior research has focused upon the "negatives"–why faculty members *do not* view librarians as "equal" partners in the academic enterprise and why the majority of faculty *do not* use LI. This emphasis on the "negatives" is perhaps justifiable, given that non-users of LI are among the majority of faculty on most campuses, but the reasons why some faculty *are* strong proponents of LI should also be explored in hopes of finding ways of transforming non-users into users. The current study examines this "positive alternative": Why do some faculty use librarian-provided instruction with their classes? And, why are they firm proponents of the educational role of libraries and librarians? Additionally, earlier studies of faculty use of LI have generally relied on selected-response survey instruments, rather than interviews, focus groups, or other constructed-response methodologies that allow faculty members to voice their concerns and rationales in their own words. The choice of options in a survey instrument particularly constrains respondents, while interviews allow them to express any and all views they are willing to share.[14] Baker (1997), who used focus groups; Leckie and Fullerton (1999), who conducted 35 interviews with faculty; and Major (1993), who interviewed 18 librarians, were unique in using non-survey devices to study faculty views of LI. Their findings are particularly illuminative and provided the major inspiration for this study, which also relies upon interviews.[15]

METHODOLOGY

Faculty selected for interviews were drawn from a database detailing all LI sessions conducted at New Mexico State University (NMSU) between 1997 and 2001. Only faculty deemed heavy LI users comprised the target population. Heavy LI users were defined as those who had requested LI sessions for multiple courses over several semesters and whose sessions were taught by different librarians. Both non-tenure-track and tenured/tenure-track faculty were included in the target population. Non-tenure track faculty, or adjuncts, were included because they are long-term employees at NMSU who regularly use LI. Excluded from the target population were faculty who requested LI infrequently or who requested LI for only a single course. Also excluded were those who always requested the same librarian for all their LI sessions. The rationale for excluding these faculty members rests with their low commitment to LI generally. Only 43 faculty members could be defined as heavy LI users by these criteria, and 30 of these 43 were randomly selected–by using a table of random numbers–for interviews.[16]

Of the 30 faculty members selected, 21 could be interviewed in the time frame given (mid-February to mid-March 2003). Table 1 provides a summary of interviewee demographics in relation to those of NMSU faculty generally (Table 1). It should be noted that the faculty group interviewed for this study was never intended as a representative sample. What is interesting, however, is that faculty interviewed came from five out of six academic colleges and that the percentages of colleges represented for each group, both interviewed faculty and total main campus faculty, are roughly similar. Another rough similarity is seen in the break-

TABLE 1. Interviewee and NMSU Main Campus Demographics

CLASSIFICATION	INTERVIEWEES		MAIN CAMPUS	
COLLEGE	*N = 21*	*% of Total*	*N = 666*	*% of Total*
Agriculture	2	10	98	15
Arts and Sciences	14	66	299	45
Business	3	14	73	11
Education	1	5	64	10
Engineering	0	0	80	12
Health and Social Services	1	5	37	6
Library	0	0	15	2
TENURE				
Tenured/Tenure-Track	16	76	549	82
Non-Tenure Track	5	24	117	18
GENDER				
Male	14	67	421	63
Female	7	33	245	37

down of gender and tenure status. Thirty-three percent of interviewees are female whereas females comprise 37 percent of all campus faculty. While 15 percent of all NMSU faculty are in the College of Agriculture, 10 percent of interviewees came from that college. The Colleges of Business, Education and Health and Social Services are also approximately represented among interviewees. Only the College of Arts and Sciences has a higher percentage of faculty interviewed (66 percent) than are found campus-wide within that college (45 percent).

Interview questions were developed with the goal of uncovering faculty values and attitudes regarding LI. Interviews were conducted over a three-week period in the middle of spring semester 2003. Most interviews lasted 30 minutes or less and were conducted in a location of the interviewee's choosing, typically their own offices. The authors conducted all interviews and asked all 21 interviewees the same six core questions:

1. Tell us about when you first began incorporating librarian-provided information research instruction into your courses and how long you have been doing this.
2. Why do you think it is important that your students be taught library research skills and information sources?

3. Why do you ask a librarian to teach your students library research skills and information sources?
4. Tell us about your best and worst experiences with librarian-provided information research instruction. What made these "best" and "worst" experiences stand out?
5. Please recall some concrete examples of library instruction that made a difference, either positively or negatively, for you and/or for your students.
6. Beyond these concrete examples, please tell us about your perceptions of the effects, either short or long term, of librarian-provided research instruction on the students in your course.

Interviewers asked follow-up questions as needed to clarify points made, to put the interview back on track, or to get the faculty member to elaborate on certain areas. Interviewers tape-recorded each interview and also took notes during the interview. Tapes were later transcribed and analyzed to find similarities or trends among the answers to each question, as well as among interviewees regardless of question. Themes figuring in faculty responses are reported in simple frequency counts. Because respondents were not required to pick a single choice, as when given options on a survey, some faculty voiced multiple themes in response to particular questions, and the total number of themes tallied in response to a question may thus exceed 21.

FINDINGS

Why Faculty Use LI

When asked why they use LI, 15 of 21 respondents noted that students lack library research skills. This was the reason cited most frequently by faculty, and it was often expressed with an awareness of students' personal backgrounds and academic preparation for college (Figure 1). One professor of government noted, "Our students come to us not necessarily having had the strongest academic backgrounds. Their high schools and hometowns may not have had a library. They may never have had to write a research paper in high school." An English professor echoed the comparative dearth of libraries in New Mexico, saying "If you think about New Mexico, the state of New Mexico still has a lot of rural high schools that do not have a school library per se. They have a county library but it's not the same as a Class I research

FIGURE 1

Interview Question 1: Why do you think it is important that students be taught library research skills and information sources?	
Students lack skills	15 of 21
Combat the Internet	15 of 21
LI needed for success in college	13 of 21
Develop students' evaluative skills	9 of 21
Future success as graduate students or employees	7 of 21
Research is hard and students need to learn how difficult it is	3 of 21
Develop students' critical thinking skills	3 of 21
Encourages lifelong learning	2 of 21
Promotes an informed citizenry	1 of 21

library." The concerns that faculty here expressed about students' lack of library and information research skills parallel findings of earlier studies: 70 percent of faculty in the studies of both Haws, Peterson and Shonrock (1989, 202) and Cannon (1994, 528) said that first-year students did not have the skills necessary to use a research library or rated the ability of these students to do research as "poor."[17] They also seem to be closely linked to another reason frequently mentioned by interviewees: 13 of 21 respondents noted that students need LI to be successful in their current academic efforts. "For history majors, you really need to be able to do a research paper. I mean, that's the basic goal of the course," said one professor.

Interviewees' comments reveal, however, some dissonance between their attitudes and those commonly expressed by, or ascribed to, faculty. These faculty certainly do not view the library as easy to use (Hardesty 1991, 8), or library research as something students will just pick up on their own. One English professor went so far as to say, "I don't know anybody who would say, 'well, students will do it on their own.' I guess we did it on our own, but things were much simpler then." They do not think students who lack research skills are simply lacking in motivation (Gonzales 2001, 197). Nor have they forgotten that "most undergraduates share neither their abilities nor their motivations" (Hardesty 1991, 104)–one history professor even said, "When I was a teenager I spent many of my weekends in libraries . . . so I'm a little not usual." They are committed to library use for all students, not just

potential graduate students (Hardesty 1991, 45). In fact, these interviewees consistently displayed the knowledge of students' backgrounds, their academic preparation, learning styles, and needs that are
characteristic of "teaching oriented" rather than "research oriented faculty" (Hardesty 1991, 75).

Fifteen of 21 respondents also mentioned using LI to "combat the
Net." One professor of business said of LI, "To me it's important because we have so much reliance on the Internet. There is a lot of information sitting in the library that is simply never going to be available on
the Web." A history professor was even more emphatic: "[LI's] importance has really increased at a monumental pace because of the Internet.
The bad part is that they [students] are ignorant of how to use a traditional library, and so as a result of that they turn to the Internet as a sub-
stitute, when they are even more ignorant of that, and so it compounds
the disaster in what was already a catastrophic situation." The "library
versus the Internet" figured prominently in interviewees' remarks and
echoed concerns about the Internet being expressed by faculty nationwide (Carlson 2003; Rothenberg 1997). Rabinowitz has noted that such
concerns may make faculty particularly receptive to LI at present: "At
the same time, however, the Web has become an unavoidable force in
the lives of most teachers and students, and teachers suddenly seem
ready to address the issues of how students go about searching for, selecting, and evaluating sources" (2000, 340).

This perceived need to combat the Internet directly ties in to the third
most frequent reason that faculty mentioned for using LI: 9 of 21 cited
students' need to develop evaluative responses to information. One
agronomy and horticulture professor explicitly framed the need for students to develop evaluative responses to information in terms of the
Internet, saying, "Anymore, all the students know how to use the
Internet, they know how to get information off the Internet. But their
discriminator sucks . . . They don't know what is good information versus bad information." A business professor echoed these concerns:
"The big concern that I have is the gullibility of students regarding the
free information available on the free Internet–their lack of cynicism
about the information they read on the free Internet." Interestingly,
though, only three of the 21 faculty members explicitly mentioned the
development of critical thinking skills either in relation to evaluative responses to information or in their general comments. Moreover, none of
the three who did mention critical thinking framed it specifically in
terms of the evaluative response to information. Rather, critical thinking was positioned as the end product of a university education: "I think

one of the things you can do at the university is to get students to think critically and, hopefully, begin to start working on some of these problems. Information is the key ingredient in the recipe to make it work," said one geography professor.

Faculty members also mentioned other factors, albeit less frequently, as to why LI was important for students. Future success in graduate school or the workplace was mentioned by 7 of 21. Three of 21 emphasized that research is difficult and students grow intellectually by confronting the difficulties of the research. Only two mentioned lifelong learning, one of the benefits of LI–and especially of information literacy–that is commonly cited by librarians. Another two mentioned that LI helps students to satisfy personal curiosity, while one mentioned that LI contributed to the development of students as citizens. Overall, interviewees' responses suggest a potential mismatch between librarians' rhetoric about LI and faculty members' reasons for valuing LI. Despite the fact that information literacy is a required component in the upper-division general education curriculum at NMSU, none of these faculty mentioned general education in relation to LI, a finding in keeping with Hardesty's claim that a "sophisticated understanding of the library and increasing competence in its use as a goal of general education is not accepted, perhaps not understood by most faculty" (Hardesty 1991, 8). Critical thinking, lifelong learning, and citizenship were, likewise, only sporadically invoked by interviewees. Rather, their rationales for using LI focused prominently on short-term, course-related needs.

Why Faculty Have a Librarian Teach LI

Eighteen out of 21 respondents described the "librarian as expert" when asked why they had a librarian provide LI for their classes (Figure 2). That this was the most frequently given response should be heartening to those worried that faculty members lack respect for librarians' knowledge. One member of the history department framed this knowledge in terms of information systems and collections, saying, "You're the experts. You know your system, you know your collections much better than I know [them]," while an English professor noted the librarians' awareness of up-to-the-minute changes, commenting, "I just don't have the expertise a librarian has and it's changing. Research is changing so rapidly that I myself feel like I'm way behind in it." Yet another interviewee–a history professor–characterized the difference between his knowledge and the librarian's in the following terms: "for me to be teaching the students how to use the library would be like having a

FIGURE 2

Interview Question 2: Why do you ask a librarian to teach your students library research skills and information sources?	
Librarian is the expert	18 of 21
Faculty want to keep up-to-date	9 of 21
Librarian validates faculty objectives for student learning	7 of 21

plumber try to teach students how to do heart surgery. . . . [W]hy have a wash-horse do it when you can turn to Secretariat?" Faculty's willingness to defer to librarians as "experts" on information research probably reflects the concern for disciplinary boundaries characteristic of faculty culture generally: "[s]pecialization dominates graduate study and faculty defer to each other based on specialization" (Hardesty 1995, 349).[18] It also betrays a more pragmatic awareness by faculty that they cannot keep up with the changes in information technologies, that–in the words of Raspa and Ward–"we have reached a point at which neither librarians nor instructional faculty can adequately teach the research process in isolation from each other" (2000, 15-16).

The second most frequent response to this question emphasized faculty members themselves being life-long learners. Nine of 21 respondents sounded variations on the following themes:

- "I can't even keep up with the databases, and I don't know anybody who would ever say, 'well students will do it own their own'" (English).
- "[T]he fact is, every time she does it, she brings up some new development. . . . I'm clearly not staying up with the developments in information technology, or information literacy or whatever you want to call it. So every time she does it she brings something new" (Education).
- "I like to learn new tricks too, so I enjoy attending the class and library workshops because I know I'll learn something" (Criminal Justice).

This finding is in keeping with the results of prior studies, which similarly noted that faculty valued librarians' help in "upgrading" their information research skills (Leckie & Fullerton 1999, 27), especially when they could then use those skills to "better teach students" (Ducas & Michaud-Oystryk 2003, 70).

Seven out of 21 respondents expressed variations on the "librarian as 'expert witness.'" This was the third most frequent response to this question and probably ties back to the most frequent response, recognition of the librarian's expertise when it comes to information systems and sources: "Students don't always believe me when [I] say something about the library. I think that having someone who works there introduce students to resources, to research, lends credibility to what they are saying," said a government professor. An English-as-a-Foreign-Language (EFL) professor echoed this view, saying, "I'll tell you, when I stand up and say these things in a class, students are a little skeptical because they're new to this system and this way of doing things. I think they think it's all my strange notion. When they hear another person from outside the classroom saying the very same thing, it's very reinforcing. They begin to see it as a big system; as a big process that pervades various parts of the university. It's not just some EFL teacher's way of making life hard for them." A history professor compared the librarian's role vis-à-vis the faculty-student relationship to that other adults sometimes play in the parent-child relationship: "[LI] just reinforces what I say. . . . [K]ids, if their parents tell them something, it goes right past them but if another adult or another person of authority tells them, it will reinforce. I'm just trying to maximize the effectiveness of what I say." It is unknown to what degree students do, in fact, find librarians' words about information sources and search strategies more persuasive than those of faculty members. Faculty members' readiness to credit this authority to librarians, though, is encouraging—and somewhat surprising, as librarians often expect faculty to play this same role, of outside authority, in their own dealings with students.

Best Experiences with LI

When asked about their best LI experiences, 11 of 21 respondents noted that the LI was specifically focused on their course content, rather than a generic session (Figure 3). This was the most frequent answer. To quote some typical responses:

- "The orientations work best when they are tailored to a class. I know that's asking a lot of the people who give them, but it also means you can't have a 'one size fits all' approach" (Government).

- "Sometimes I get something that's a little too general and . . . too basic for what my students need. . . .I don't usually take them over there unless they need something specific" (English).

Interviewees' words here provide a good reminder of Leckie and Fullerton's warning that "a library research program will not succeed if it is kept generic" (1999, 27).[19] This finding may be quite significant to the development of library instruction programs. Information literacy instruction, in particular, has focused upon providing students with general skills (such as understanding the distinction between keyword and subject searching), rather than particular knowledge (such as the exact Library of Congress subject headings that one should use in a library catalog to find books on the history of Communism in Eastern Europe). Faculty, however, seem to value the latter form of instruction more highly than the former.

The second most frequent description of their "best" LI session compared the LI session to hyper reference service. Ten of 21 respondents expressed variations on this theme. A government professor said, "Getting actual librarian assistance is the most helpful part of library instruction. If you give them specific topics, they will help you focus in right away on that topic area, material for it, finding sources. It's just like at the reference desk," while a business professor said, "I think the library sessions are pretty much in the can and how your people distinguish themselves is one-on-one with my students because that's so time-consuming." That faculty characterized their best LI session(s) in terms of reference confirms that faculty really value librarians' reference work.

FIGURE 3

Interview Question 3:		
Tell us about your best and worst experiences with librarian-provided research instruction. What made these "best" and "worst" experiences stand out?		

Best experiences		**Worst experiences**	
Instruction is tied to specific assignment	11 of 21	Librarian and students not connecting in class	12 of 21
Librarian provides in-depth reference assistance to students in class	10 of 21	Librarian and faculty not communicating/collaborating	8 of 21
Students receive hands-on experience with print and electronic sources	9 of 21	Information overload	5 of 21

Studies have found that faculty interact more with librarians in reference than in any other area (e.g., collection development) (Ducas & Michaud-Oystryk 2003, 59). The blending of LI and reference here suggests, however, that faculty do not necessarily view reference as "just service"; rather, it seems to be conceptualized as a venue for individualized learning.

Six of 21 respondents mentioned both the hands-on nature of their "best" LI session and the subject knowledge of the librarian-instructor, tying these for third place in the frequency of responses to this question. Interestingly, in emphasizing the hands-on nature of the LI sessions, more faculty members mentioned students' manipulations of print resources than computer databases. One English professor said, "Actually bringing in print resources for a topic and showing those, letting them handle those, was so important," while an EFL professor similarly commented, "The [sessions] that are really good are when students not only access information from the electronic article databases but when librarians also bring in hard copies of things." This concern for students' handling of print materials could perhaps be viewed as an extension of the conception of the "library as treasure house" and the concomitant view that "just having books, lots of books, positively influences students" that Hardesty found characteristic of faculty culture (Hardesty 1991, 45). It more probably, though, ties in to interviewees' expressed worries about student reliance on the Internet and a desire to familiarize them with other information media. Many of these faculty seem genuinely to love books or journals in their fields and want to share their passion for these sources with their students.

The librarian's knowledge of the subject was invoked with equal frequency as the hands-on nature of the instruction. As one history professor said of the librarian who taught his "best" LI session, "You know something about the [history of the] southwest, so you can give information to the students." Librarians' lack of knowledge was cited by faculty in several prior surveys as one of the reasons they did not use LI, and librarians at many institutions have worked concertedly to acquire disciplinary degrees and have them valued by faculty (Divay, Ducas & Michaud-Oystryk 1987, 31). What is interesting about the responses in these interviews, however, is that in only one case did the librarian whose knowledge was mentioned as contributing to the "best" LI session of a particular faculty member have a graduate degree in the subject field of the course. This suggests that librarians are valued for their disciplinary knowledge–as information scientists–of information resources,[20] or that the knowledge of a field they acquire from working with students, faculty, and these resources is seen as sufficient. One history professor described how he could bring a librarian lacking knowledge of the subject area up to speed: "First of all, you go over to the librarian's office and talk to them. Say "What are you going to do in the session? Are you going to have handouts? What kind of information would you like from me? What can I offer? . . . Maybe it would take two or more sessions with the librarian before the actual classroom presentation." This quote exemplifies something that appears several times in the interviews–a "light bulb moment" for the faculty member as s/he realizes that advance collaboration with librarians in preparing LI could produce a better result for the students.

Other factors mentioned in the description of their "best" LI session were the technological capabilities of the classroom (6 of 21 respondents); the librarians' preparations for the session (3 of 21 respondents); the librarians' in-class interactions with the students (2 of 21 respondents); librarian-developed worksheets for the session (2 of 21 respondents); the librarian's creating a Web page for the class (1 of 21 respondents); and the librarian's commitment to students (1 of 21 respondents).

Worst Experiences with LI

Disconnects between the librarian and the students and between the librarian and the course instructor figured prominently in faculty members' descriptions of their "worst" LI sessions. Twelve of 21 respondents mentioned a disconnect between librarians and students, making it the most frequently given response. As one English professor noted, "If the instructor is not enthusiastic, the students just turn off and then the instructor gets more frustrated and the students pick up on this and the situation just keeps getting worse. It becomes a vicious circle."

An EFL professor said, "My worst experience was taking a guided tour with a librarian. This person had no concept of how to adjust her own language to the needs of non-native speakers. The students were rolling their eyes and panicking and I was embarrassed."

A disconnection between the librarian and the faculty member was the second most frequently mentioned theme in descriptions of the "worst" LI sessions. Eight of 21 respondents mentioned misdirection, with librarians and course instructors giving students different instructions; miscommunication, with librarians and course instructors failing to understand one another in planning the session; or mismatches in instructional approaches between librarians and faculty. Faculty were especially frustrated when librarians' directions to students contradicted their own instructions to their classes. One finance professor described her unhappiness when librarians told her students to use Lexis-Nexis instead of Westlaw, whose use she had specified, in completing an assignment. Lack of communication in planning LI sessions also factored prominently in descriptions of "worst" LI sessions. As one finance professor said, "The further that I work in advance to talk to someone at the library about what I want, the better aligned what I got was with what I wanted. And I guess that is just because people can't read your minds but if you don't tell them exactly what you are after it's hard to deliver." A history professor likewise commented, "I was doing things on . . . Russia, and she didn't know anything about Russia . . . I think the problem was that I should have interacted more with her to prepare the session. She did sort of a generic thing." Differences in teaching styles were also mentioned. One English professor noted that some librarians seem to prefer more controlled and quiet classrooms than he would use: "So we have a tomb? Some of the librarians there seem to want this, not the library as a laboratory, a learning environment, a classroom. No– that could be noisy and messy." Speaking about a librarian's questionable use of the time during an instruction session, a business professor said, "There's so much in my classes that I try to pack in every minute that I don't have time for that."

These comments confirm the need for librarians to have a "flexible pedagogic approach" (Leckie & Fullerton 1999, 27) and to adapt their teaching style to that of the faculty with whom they work. Librarians should also remember that faculty expect to be held accountable, by their students, for what the librarian does in the classroom. As one English professor said of a "bad" LI session: "The students just lose interest and they resent my taking their time to bring them over there."

Time constraints in the LI session were mentioned by 5 of 21 respondents, making it the third most frequent response. "I know that I had one librarian doing a program during the Business Administration 211 who was just determined to do some online stuff and the online system was slow. It was painful for me to watch and sit silently by while they let the minutes tick by," said one business professor. A government professor likewise commented, "So maybe the less successful orientations are those that try to cover too much in a short space of time," and an education professor said that a particular librarian "always struck me as feeling this compulsion to give as much information as possible to the students. I always felt that it was more than most of us could digest."

The only other response given–by two of 21 respondents–focused on technology failures during the LI session.

Faculty Perceptions of LI's Impact on Students

The most frequently mentioned benefit of LI was increased efficiency in students' research (Figure 4). Fifteen of 21 respondents gave comments such as the following:

- "The Internet . . . That can take a lot of time and you can get very little results unless you have some guidance" (Government).
- "For graduate students, the short term effect is that it really does speed up their process" (Agronomy and Horticulture).
- "I'd hope that students would do better academic work because they've learned to do things more efficiently. Efficiency in work is important, it's important in the library–you need to be able to get in, get what you need, and get out" (Government).

This response confirms a finding by Ducas and Michaud-Oystryk that "all faculty . . . reported that the main result of consulting a librarian was that it saved time" (2003, 68). Faculty value strong library and information research skills because when students have these they can find information quickly for whatever needs they have–writing papers, delivering speeches, conducting laboratory experiments or field research. The frequency with which faculty used various words describing expeditious research was striking (28 times by 15 respondents), although social sciences and sciences faculty expressed such sentiments more often than humanities faculty.

Ten of 21 respondents mentioned that LI both leads to better products–papers and presentations–from students and opens "new worlds" to them, tying these for the position of second most frequently given response. In terms of LI leading to better products, faculty said:

- "They get better assignments and they do better on exams" (Economics);
- "I think it's definitely increasing the value of the research assignments that they are coming out with" (English);
- "Overall, library instruction makes it easier for us to do our jobs, to teach composition, because it gives students a basis to write from" (English).

FIGURE 4

Interview Questions 4 and 5: Could you recall some concrete examples of library instruction experiences that made a difference (positively or negatively) for you and/or your students? Could you tell us your preconceptions of the effects, either short or long term, of librarian-provided research instruction on the students in your course?	
Increased efficiency research	15 of 21
Students produce better products	10 of 21
Students are more comfortable with libraries and research process	7 of 21

LI is also valued for opening "new worlds" to students: "At the undergraduate level, it's simply trying to generate that sense of discovery and interest in students. They've gone to the university and if I'm successful I've provided them lots of opportunities to learn," said a geography professor. A history professor noted, "To realize that there is this whole treasure chest of books there on almost any topic that they want, just available for their reading. That's just opening up a whole new world for them." A few faculty were less confident that LI's impact on their students could be proven by the students' products but nevertheless remained strong supporters of the LI process generally. One English professor thus said, "I would like to say that I see much better papers out of it [LI]. I'm not sure that's the case . . . a lot of it is just faith, you know, and . . . belief in the process." No faculty interviewed could offer empirical "proof" that LI had contributed to better student work, but like faculty in earlier studies, they "saw evidence," in students' work that proved persuasive to them (Cannon 1994, 537; Leckie & Fullerton 1999, 23).

The third most frequently cited benefit of LI–mentioned by 7 of 21 respondents–was that it increases students' comfort with libraries and research. "At least the students see a librarian [whom] they may recognize later [and] they may not be intimidated in asking questions later," said a finance professor. An education professor said that prior to the instruction session "there was a terrible feeling of insecurity" among students. An English professor similarly commented, "I think what happens is that it becomes more manageable for students, less stressful." Faculty's concern about students' comfort in the library is heartening because it is, again, an indication of "teaching-oriented" rather than "research-oriented" faculty. As Mellon's study (1986) and its successors have shown, "library anxiety" is a very real phenomenon, with as many as 75-85 percent of students expressing feelings of fear or anxiety in relation to library use, and it can preclude successful library use.

Interviewees' comments, however, reveal another potential disconnect between librarians' discourse about LI and that of faculty. Librarians are very concerned that LI meet cognitive goals and objectives and not be just a "feel-good" orientation. Faculty, however, may see value in a library session that meets goals and objectives in the affective rather than the cognitive domain. Baker also found that faculty view "library use skills" as an important way to help increase the self-esteem and self-confidence of students" (1997, 181).

When Faculty Began Using LI

Fifteen of 21 respondents said they first began using LI with their courses because they began teaching a course–typically a research methods course–already on the books or developed by another. This was the most frequently mentioned response (Figure 5). Personal contact with a librarian was the second most frequently mentioned response, given by 9 of 21 respondents. The value of personal contacts in increasing faculty receptiveness to LI has been noted in much previous research (Carlson 2003; Ducas & Michaud-Oystryk 2003, 73; Hardesty 1991, 6) and highlights the importance of librarians' liaison programs, outreach efforts, and participation in campus governance. As Divay, Ducas, and Michaud-Oystryk found in their study, the "results strongly suggest that faculty members who have interacted with librarians have a better understanding of their functions and the usefulness of their expertise" (1987, 32). Some of the librarians who were specifically men-

FIGURE 5

Interview Question 6: When did you first begin incorporating librarian-provided research instruction into your courses?	
Required by course taught	15 of 21
Personal contact with librarian	9 of 21
Bitten by LI bug elsewhere	7 of 21

tioned by interviewees possess the "long history at an institution" that some have described as conducive to librarian-faculty collaboration (Major 1993, 466). Other librarians, however, had been at the institution for comparatively shorter time periods (2-5 years) but comport themselves with the self-confidence in their own identity as faculty and this behavior has also been described as conducive to librarian-faculty collaboration (Hardesty 1995, 360; Major 1993, 466). Five of 21 respondents noted that they first became involved with LI at another institution, often when they were graduate students.

CONCLUSIONS

While certain common themes definitely emerged from these interviews, faculty's responses also displayed a range that would make it difficult, if not impossible, to fashion a unified rationale for an instruction program's course-integration initiatives that would be universally persuasive. For example, some faculty very much value hands-on interaction with print resources; others expressed no preferences in this area. Similarly, although three faculty mentioned critical thinking in their comments, the majority did not. It is also significant that there was only one voicing of the specific term, *information literacy*, in the course of all 21 interviews and this was by an education professor. This may indicate that librarians should keep in mind that there is a certain "disconnect" in both terminology and concepts between *what faculty want* and what librarians perceive that their students *need* from library instruction. All this suggests that, as Hardesty previously noted, "Proponents of bibliographic instruction seeking a 'royal road' for faculty adoption of bibliographic instruction will be disappointed" (Hardesty 1995, 361). [21] Rather, librarians should listen to the expressions, and thus the values, of individual faculty members on their campuses and situate the benefits of LI in relation to these values. In addition to variation among faculty on a campus, it is also expected that there could be even greater variation between faculty on different campuses (Hardesty 1991, 29 & 1995, 359). As Hightower suggests, though, "Identifying attitudes is a significant step toward designing outreach programs directed at increased use of the library" (Hightower 1996, 4), and librarians would be well served for similar research projects uncovering faculty attitudes on their own campuses.

NOTES

1. Faculty themselves recognize this; see Starkey (1974, 175). More recently, see Baker (1997, 177) and Hardesty (1995, 342). Awareness of this has prompted much disquiet among librarians (Hardesty 1995, 340-341; Feldman & Sciammarella 2000, 491; and Lipow 1991, 7 & 10).

2. See Divay, Ducas and Michaud-Oystryk (1987), Ducas and Michaud-Oystryk (2003), Hardesty (1995), and Lipow (1991).

3. Librarians in this study were, however, rated highly for helping faculty in *their* instructional activities (Ivey 1994, 72). See also Stahl (1997, 134).

4. While 21 percent of respondents in this survey credited librarians with "very substantial involvement in the educational process," another 37 percent felt that "librarians had no involvement at all in their students' education" (Divay, Ducas & Michaud-Oystryk 1987, 31). Similar findings are reported by Amstutz and Whitson (1997, 23), but those of Ivey (1994, 74) are contradictory.

5. For similar findings, see Amstutz and Whitson (1997, 23) and Leckie and Fullerton (1999, 14 & 24).

6. Demographic factors have been explored in relation to faculty's willingness to incorporate LI into their courses, with various–and sometimes inconclusive–findings correlating faculty members' receptiveness to LI to age, teaching experience, highest degree, source of highest degree, type of courses taught, experiences in learning library use, frequency of library use, publishing output, general satisfaction with the library, sex, class size, suitability of materials for specific courses, views of students' research skills, discipline, course level. See Boosinger 1990; Cannon 1994; Gonzales 2001; Hardesty 1991 and 1995; Ivey 1994; Thomas 1994; and Thomas and Ensor 1984.

7. This is especially common among science and engineering faculty teaching beginning courses (Leckie and Fullerton 1999, 17).

8. While only 16 percent of the faculty at California State, Long Beach, selected this option in 1982, 52.5 percent did in 1990 (Thomas 1994, 213).

9. Interestingly, Sinn found that while "[s]ome [biology] faculty may feel their depth of subject knowledge is required for proper instruction" (2000, 24), there is actually little difference between topics in LI provided by librarians and that provided by faculty (2000, 32).

10. See also Gonzales 2001, 198 and Sinn 2000, 24.

11. See also Feldman and Sciammarella 2000, 494; Hightower 1996, 5; Thomas 1994, 216.

12. See also Amstutz and Whitson 1997, 19 and 24; Hightower 1996, 5; Thomas 1994, 212 and 216-217.

13. Thomas found that only 19 of her 542 respondents indicated that they had learned library skills from a librarian lecture (1994, 213). See also Hightower 1996, 16 and Maynard 1990, 72.

14. An additional problem with surveys is that respondents may well select particular options without subscribing to the views that researchers then ascribe to them based upon their choices. For example, respondents saying that they interacted most frequently with librarians in a reference capacity, not an instructional one, might not agree that they valued librarians most for their "service" roles.

15. Concern with demographic factors that correlate with faculty receptiveness to LI yields data valuable in its predictiveness, but lacking in transformative potential.

Faculty members' age, highest degree, etc. are not subject to change, even if they are found to correlate strongly with receptiveness to LI.

16. The table of random numbers used with this study is that found in Fink (1995, 28).

17. See also Gonzales (2001, 194).

18. See Major (1993, 467) on those "mature" librarians who described their relationships with faculty in terms of disciplinary equality: "As one subject observed, 'We are equal. They represent a discipline, and I represent a discipline–a mutual type of thing.'"

19. See also Baker (1997, 181), who notes that "broad strategies aimed at inducing faculty to make student library assignments are not as likely to yield positive results as are strategies tailored to faculty's specific pedagogical concerns."

20. Yang interestingly found that "having the subject background to serve as a research consultant" ranked 8th of 10 options in one survey of faculty members' attitudes toward the importance of services provided by library liaisons (2000, 126).

21. Cannon makes a similar point, having found in her study that "no one model [of LI] was given this highest rating by more than 50 percent of faculty. This suggests that it would be a mistake to try to force one instruction model on all faculty" (1994, 533).

REFERENCES

Amstutz, Donna and Whitson, Donna. (1997). University faculty and information literacy: Who teaches the students? *Research Strategies, 15* (1), 18-25.

Baker, Robert K. (1997). Faculty perceptions toward student library use in a large urban community college. *Journal of Academic Librarianship, 23* (3), 177-182.

Boosinger, Marcia L. (1990). Associations between faculty publishing output and opinions regarding student library skills. *College & Research Libraries, 51*, 471-481.

Boyer Commission on Educating Undergraduates in the Research University. (2002). *Reinventing undergraduate education: Three years after the Boyer report.* Available at: <www.sunysb.edu/pres/0210066-Boyer%20Report%20Final.pdf>.

Cannon, Anita. (1994). Faculty survey of library research instruction. *RQ, 33*, 524-541.

Carlson, Scott. (2003, March 21). New allies in the fight against research by Googling. *Chronicle of Higher Education.* Available at http://chronicle.com/weekly/v49/i28/28a03301.htm.

Divay, Gaby, Ducas, Ada M., and Michaud-Oystryk, Nicole. (1987). Faculty perceptions of librarians at the University of Manitoba. *College & Research Libraries, 48*, 27-35.

Ducas, Ada M. and Michaud-Oystryk, Nicole. (2003). Toward a new enterprise: Capitalizing on the faculty/librarian partnership. *College & Research Libraries, 64* (1), 55-74.

Feldman, Devin and Sciammarella, Susan. (2000). Both sides of the looking glass: Librarian and teaching faculty perceptions of librarianship at six community colleges. *College & Research Libraries, 61* (6), 491-498.

Fink, Arlene. (1995). *How to design surveys.* Thousand Oaks, CA: Sage Publications.

Gonzales, Rhonda. (2001). Opinions and experiences of university faculty regarding library research instruction: Results of a Web-based survey at the University of Southern Colorado. *Research Strategies, 18*, 191-201.

Hardesty, Larry. (1995). Faculty culture and bibliographic instruction: An exploratory analysis. *Library Trends, 44* (2), 339-367.

Hardesty, Larry. (1991). *Faculty and the library: The undergraduate experience.* Norwood, NJ: Ablex Publishing, 1991.

Haws, Rae, Peterson, Lorna, and Shonrock, Diana. (1989, March). Survey of faculty attitudes towards a basic library skills course. *College and Research Libraries News,* no. 3, 201-203.

Hightower, Barbara. (1996). *The effect of faculty library attitudes and experiences on undergraduate use of the geology library at the University of North Carolina at Chapel Hill.* Master's thesis.

Ivey, Robert T. (1994). Teaching faculty perceptions of academic librarians at Memphis State University. *College & Research Libraries, 55*, 69-82.

Knapp, Patricia B. (1958). College teaching and the library. *Illinois Libraries, 40*, 828-833.

Leckie, Gloria J. and Fullerton, Anne. (1999). Information literacy in science and engineering undergraduate education: Faculty attitudes and pedagogical practices. *College & Research Libraries, 60* (1), 9-29.

Lipow, Anne G. (1991). Outreach to faculty: Why and how. *In Working with faculty in the new electronic library* (pp. 7-13). Ann Arbor, MI: Pierian Press.

Lubans, John. (1980). Library Literacy: Let George Do It. *RQ, 20,* 121-23.

Major, Jean Armour. (1993). Mature librarians and the university faculty: Factors contributing to librarians' acceptance as colleagues. *College & Research Libraries, 54*, 463-469.

Maynard, J. Edmund. (1990). A case study of faculty attitudes toward library instruction: The Citadel experience. *Reference Services Review, 18* (2), 67-76.

Mellon, Constance A. (1986). Library anxiety: A grounded theory and its development. *College & Research Libraries, 47*, 160-5.

Rabinowitz, Celia. (2000). Working in a vacuum: A study of the literature of student research and writing. *Research Strategies, 17*, 337-346.

Raspa, Dick and Ward, Dane. (2000). Listening for collaboration: Faculty and librarians working together. In Dick Raspa and Dane Ward (Eds.), *The collaborative imperative: Librarians and faculty working together in the information universe* (pp. 1-18). Chicago: Association of College and Research Libraries.

Rothenberg, David. (1997, August 15). How the Web destroys the quality of students' research papers. *Chronicle of Higher Education,* PAGE.

Sellen, Mary K. and Jirouch, Jan. (1984). Perceptions of library use by faculty and students: A comparison. *College & Research Libraries, 45*, 259-267.

Sinn, Robin N. (2000). A comparison of library instruction content by biology faculty and librarians. *Research Strategies, 17*, 23-34.

Stahl, Aletha D. "What I want in a librarian": One new faculty member's perspective. *Reference & User Services Quarterly, 37* (2), 133-135.

Starkey, John D. (1974). Library-use instruction: A college teacher's viewpoint. In *Educating the library user* (pp. 175-180). New York: Bowker.

Thomas, Joy. (1994). Faculty attitudes and habits concerning library instruction: How much has changed since 1982? *Research Strategies, 12* (4), 209-223.

Thomas, Joy and Ensor, Pat. (1984). University faculty and library instruction. *RQ, 23,* 431-437.

Yang, Zheng Ye. (2000). University faculty's perception of a library liaison program: A case study. *Journal of Academic Librarianship, 26* (2), 124-128.

The Library Liaison Toolkit:
Learning to Bridge
the Communication Gap

Stephan J. Macaluso
Barbara Whitney Petruzzelli

SUMMARY. SUNY New Paltz established a library liaison program in 2001, long after such programs were commonplace at many U.S. college and university libraries. The program emerged, not simply from a desire to enhance library service, but because library faculty came to view it as a multi-faceted mechanism capable of addressing multiple concerns. The new library-wide initiative demanded high-level communication skills, an in-depth understanding of library policies and collection development practices, and increased knowledge about individual departments and the college. A collection of campus information resources and liaison training sessions, collectively called The Library Liaison Toolkit, was developed to build liaison expertise in these areas. *[Article copies available for a fee from The Haworth Document Delivery Service: 1-800-HAWORTH. E-mail address: <docdelivery@haworthpress.com> Website: <http://www.HaworthPress.com> © 2005 by The Haworth Press, Inc. All rights reserved.]*

Stephan J. Macaluso (E-mail: macaluss@newpaltz.edu) is Distance Learning Librarian, and Barbara Whitney Petruzzelli (E-mail: petruzzb@newpaltz.edu) is Assistant Library Director, both at Sojourner Truth Library, State University of New York at New Paltz, 75 South Manheim Boulevard, New Paltz, NY 12561.

[Haworth co-indexing entry note]: "The Library Liaison Toolkit: Learning to Bridge the Communication Gap." Macaluso, Stephan J., and Barbara Whitney Petruzzelli. Co-published simultaneously in *The Reference Librarian* (The Haworth Information Press, an imprint of The Haworth Press, Inc.) No. 89/90, 2005, pp. 163-177; and: *Relationships Between Teaching Faculty and Teaching Librarians* (ed: Susan B. Kraat) The Haworth Information Press, an imprint of The Haworth Press, Inc., 2005, pp. 163-177. Single or multiple copies of this article are available for a fee from The Haworth Document Delivery Service [1-800-HAWORTH, 9:00 a.m. - 5:00 p.m. (EST). E-mail address: docdelivery@haworthpress.com].

KEYWORDS. Library liaison, training, communication, collection development, faculty relationships, model, retreat, assessment, outreach

In the late 1990s, a pair of nagging issues were surfacing with troubling regularity at Sojourner Truth Library (STL). On the one hand, librarians were chagrined at faculty's and students' lack of awareness of library resources and services. Though newsletters, flyers, and e-mails were frequently and widely distributed, many on campus didn't seem to be getting the message about the new and powerful resources that the library offered. Perceptions of collection quality also suffered. Despite relatively healthy acquisitions expenditures, library users continued to maintain that our books were old and failed to cover many current topics.

The second issue was collection development. The acquisitions budget wasn't being spent on time, resulting in a rush at the end of each fiscal year to encumber funds. Part of the reason for the slow rate of expenditure was that too few librarians and faculty were involved in selecting materials. Within the library faculty, collection development was vested heavily with the collection development coordinator, with the help of reference librarians in certain subject areas. Within the classroom faculty, there appeared to be an enduring myth that the library had no money. Despite a designated collection development contact person in each academic department, the faculty at large didn't seem to be getting the message that their acquisitions suggestions were welcome. Involvement in selection fluctuated greatly from department to department.

These matters were the subject of growing concern and conversation among New Paltz librarians. Various ideas were suggested to improve both problem areas. More publicity was needed. Marketing messages should be targeted to specific groups of library users and be frequently repeated. Faculty should be strongly encouraged to make acquisitions requests. More librarians should participate in materials selection. While the solutions were becoming clear, the path(s) to achieving them were not.

BUILDING RELATIONSHIPS

For some time, we had recognized the importance of increased interaction between classroom and library faculty and the critical role that our relationships with faculty played. A number of articles written at the time underscored the need to develop positive, ongoing relationships with campus colleagues outside the library. Donald H. Dilmore observed that "the measure of interpersonal contact was one of the strongest predictors of faculty perceptions and use of library services . . . Of the campuses studied, those where library service appeared to be most valued by the faculty were those on which librarians reported the most frequent interaction with faculty members" (Dilmore, 1996, 282-283). Deborah Jakubs concluded that "it is the personal contacts that people have with librarians that cause them to form opinions about the library" (Jakubs, 1999, 75).

Liaison programs are a popular device for increasing librarian-faculty interaction. One had never been instituted at New Paltz, primarily because of concerns about workload. It was assumed that such a program would be the sole purview of reference and instruction librarians. Throughout STL, librarians questioned whether sufficient benefit would result from the effort entailed in establishing and maintaining a major new service. Consequently, a liaison program had not been pursued.

In early 1999, STL was heavily involved in planning for the introduction of the ERes electronic course reserve system. Because the new system would have a direct impact on faculty's work processes and routines, a critical part of the ERes marketing plan was communicating to faculty. The last phase of faculty communications was meeting with each department to demonstrate the system and review new procedures. Since there were many departments to meet with in a short amount of time, STL librarians agreed that we would all participate by volunteering for a few departments each.

Some librarians approached the ERes meetings with trepidation. Would our presentation skills be up to the job? Would we know the system well enough to answer faculty questions with confidence? Would the faculty be annoyed by the change and be cranky at the meetings? Despite these concerns, we recognized electronic course reserves as a core library service and realized that its introduction wasn't just a circulation job or a systems job. All library faculty had a role in ensuring as successful an implementation as possible. With the support of the ERes project team, each STL librarian signed up for a few departments and prepared for the meetings.

Meeting outcomes exceeded our expectations. In many instances, the system demo took just a fraction of the time that the librarian spent with the department. Faculty asked questions about all kinds of topics relating to the library: acquisitions, interlibrary loan, the library Web page, hours, etc. One or two festering problems were uncovered. And many compliments were received. We were surprised to discover how much we learned from the meetings and how receptive most departments were to talking with us. The ERes meetings proved that public service experience was not required to effectively communicate with a department.

LISTENING TO LIBRARY USERS

Later in the same year, STL reinvigorated its assessment activities. We recognized that we had to listen to library users in order to make improvements that would best meet their needs. By late 1999, plans for large scale student and faculty satisfaction surveys were underway. These would be administered in 2000. Not much had been done to survey library effectiveness since 1995. With a library assessment planning committee working to establish on-going assessment, the staff as a whole took its first steps toward building a "culture of assessment." We began to try to find a place for the voice of library users, or "customers" as Shelley Phipps describes them (Phipps, 2001), in deliberations about how to change and improve library service.

Student survey results were analyzed in mid-2000. Though overall satisfaction was high, we saw some familiar problems in the deficiencies cited by students. The need for more and newer books and journals was one of their top concerns and students demonstrated low use and awareness of services/resources such as research consultations, the new-books shelf, government documents, online reference, and several others.

Mid-year 2000 also brought the close of the fiscal year and another scramble for year-end expenditures. The library faculty realized that action must be taken to stop this familiar scenario. How could we achieve broader participation in selection by both librarians and classroom faculty? We also grappled with student survey results. How could we improve perceptions of collection quality and increase awareness of underutilized resources? Would several new initiatives be required to meet these multiple demands? As conversations continued, a common thread slowly appeared.

Improved communication lay at the heart of any program we could envision to address the problems we faced. We needed a mechanism that could send targeted messages to different discipline areas as needed. We needed to be responsive to the feedback from our messages. We also needed to be able to get departmental information back to the library. What curricular changes were taking place? Who teaches which courses? If we could establish a flexible, two-way channel of communication between the library and the academic departments, we might be able to make progress on multiple fronts.

A LIBRARY RETREAT

A full-day retreat for all librarians was scheduled to explore various approaches to enhancing communication with faculty. Goals for the retreat were developed, along with issues to discuss, and possible desired outcomes (Figure 1). A trained facilitator, a librarian unaffiliated with SUNY New Paltz, agreed to finalize the agenda (Figure 2) and lead the day's discussion.

A wide-ranging conversation about the positive and negative aspects of our current communication practices brought to the forefront many of the issues we had acknowledged in earlier conversations (Figure 3). It became clear that formalized, frequent communication with academic departments had the best chance of successfully resolving the persistent problems of lack of student and faculty awareness of library resources, low faculty and librarian participation in collection development, and inadequate knowledge of faculty needs and expectations.

A consensus emerged that a liaison program could be the best way to establish formal and systematic channels of communication with faculty. By assigning librarians on an on-going basis as contact persons for a department or departments, we could target a department's specific needs and channel feedback to the library. Liaisons could promote library resources and services, encourage participation in collection development, and respond to faculty questions. Internally, they could select materials in their assigned disciplines, act as a resource in the library for those subjects, and possibly take on instruction and Web page responsibilities.

LIAISON PROGRAM WORKING MODEL

A working model of the program was drafted during the retreat. While librarians recognized the need and potential for this program, it was agreed that participation would be voluntary. Liaison activities would include communication with faculty (in-person and through a variety of other approaches); selection of library materials in all formats,

FIGURE 1. Proposed Goals, Issues, and Outcomes for Librarians' Retreat

Goals:
• Improve communication with classroom faculty on a one-to-one basis
• Fulfill our mission as a "user-centered" library
• Define the relationships between collection development and other library services
• Define core professional responsibilities
• Identify current distribution of workload
• Maintain a balance between books, journals, and other formats
• Expend our budget efficiently and wisely

Issues (agenda items):
• What works now? (e.g., examples of how to communicate with faculty now)
• Scope (contact both full-time and part-time faculty?)
• What will be obstacles and resistance? (e.g., department culture)
• What skills will be required to implement a new model?
• Workload consideration-prioritization of work, time management, etc.

Possible outcomes:
• Agree on some kind of model
• Agree on the level of commitment
• Timeline
• Workshops and training
• How to implement it? (Steps, allocations for selectors, staffing, etc.)
• Who will be responsible for the implementation?

FIGURE 2. Agenda for Library Faculty Retreat

Purpose: Enhance library/academic department communication

Desired Outcomes:
• Develop a working model for collection development/faculty communication
• Agree on a strategy for implementing the model

Agenda

Meeting Setup
Current Collection Development / Faculty Communication Practices
Working Model for Collection Development / Faculty Communication
Lunch
Working Model for Collection Development/Faculty Communication
Develop Strategy for Implementing the Model
Next Steps
Meeting Wrap-up

as well as weeding; becoming knowledgeable of and staying informed about assigned department(s); identifying disciplinary resources for the library Web page; conducting library instruction and research consultations for the department(s); acting as a contact person within the library for questions pertaining to the department(s); and referring faculty questions to others in the library as appropriate.

FIGURE 3. Communication Issues Revealed at Library Faculty Retreat

What Works	What Doesn't Work
• Faculty relationships built through library instruction classes.	• Library doesn't know faculty expectations for library collection or services.
• The ERes model: assigning librarians to work with specific departments to introduce new services.	• Some academic departments don't respond to faculty-wide invitations to participate in collection development.
• Liaison-type relationships already established with 1 or 2 departments.	• Relationships with individual faculty are built by happenstance–through instruction contacts or campus committee meetings.
• Excellent internal communication among librarians and support staff.	• Library doesn't know enough about changes taking place in departments, forcing librarians to be reactive rather than proactive.
• We learn a lot about faculty needs through the personal relationships librarians have established, through whatever channels, with faculty members.	• Faculty don't know enough about changes in the library collection, either for their own uses or to encourage student use of these resources.

One of the key elements of the program was our agreement that each liaison could work with his or her department(s) in the ways that worked best for the librarian and the department. Not every liaison activity would be relevant for every department. We defined core components to be communication, materials selection, and making referrals within the library. Other activities would be left to the discretion of the librarian. The decision to keep roles loose was key to getting buy-in from the library faculty. Librarians without regular teaching or Web page responsibilities could participate in the program without having to learn substantial new sets of skills. Nevertheless, we recognized, and the literature demonstrated, that training for liaisons would be essential (Mozenter, 2000).

Volunteers stepped forward to form a Library Liaison Working Group (LLWG). The LLWG would be responsible for drafting a working plan for the program, addressing training needs, identifying participants, and implementing a pilot program. The LLWG was made up of several librarians (many of whom had acted as unofficial liaisons for some time), the collection development librarian, and a support staff member from the Collection Development office. The assistant director of the library chaired the group.

The LLWG synthesized the observations and imperatives that had been communicated by the library faculty. It devised a set of internal and public responsibilities to be undertaken by liaisons (Figure 4). While most responsibilities would be required, it was understood that not every role would be of equal importance to each assigned department.

FIGURE 4. Library Liaison Responsibilities, November 2000

I. PUBLIC ROLE OF LIAISON

A. Communicate with faculty/departments–Liaison librarians (LL) are encouraged to:
1. Attend department/organizational meetings and meet with individual faculty as appropriate.
2. Assess needs of faculty, especially new faculty. This can be done in a variety of ways, e.g., surveys, conversation, familiarity with departmental curriculum, etc.
3. Invite faculty to the library, hold orientation sessions as needed.
4. Work with departments to support curriculum and new endeavors (e.g., new areas of study, accreditation).
5. Attend departmental functions (e.g., lectures, workshops) when possible.
6. Refer departmental needs and requests to other liaisons and STL departments as needed.

B. Promote STL resources and services
1. Notify department of new, pertinent resources and services and changes to services. (Method left up to the liaison. Working group suggests consistent, multiple means of communication, which may include e-mail, campus/snail mail, personal visits to department, new books lists.)
2. Create blurbs describing new resources/services for STL and other publications, e.g., library Web site, library, departmental and college newsletters, campus TV, etc.

C. Involve academic department in collection development
1. Encourage faculty participation in selection of new resources.
   a. Include all formats (e.g., monographs, serials, multimedia).
   b. Inform faculty of ordering procedures and options (e.g., sending requests to LL, to Collection Development, using online form, sending publishers' catalogs, library mailbox in department, etc.).
   c. Encourage faculty review and selection of pertinent Web sites. (These resources may be added to STL Web site.)
   d. Develop relationship with Collection Development contact person in assigned department.

II. INTERNAL LIAISON FUNCTIONS

A. Keep abreast of new resources and services of interest to assigned department(s).

B. Report departmental concerns and questions back to STL. Refer requests (e.g., instruction, technology, etc.) to appropriate staff members.

C. Keep STL faculty and staff apprised of important news about assigned department(s).

D. Select books, serials, and multimedia in assigned department(s).
1. Review Choice cards promptly.
2. Monitor an internal, unofficial benchmark (in dollars or titles).
3. Use other selection tools as appropriate. Become familiar with collection development resources in assigned field(s).
4. Weed relevant collections as needed on an on-going basis.

E. Contribute to STL Web page, as desired:
   Possible methods:
1. Forward suggestions for links or other resources to Web Working Group.
2. Maintain appropriate "Resources by Subject" page(s).

F. Attend library liaison meetings.

BUILDING THE LIAISON TOOLKIT

The LLWG recognized that liaisons needed to develop their abilities to communicate effectively with their assigned departments. Librarians needed ready access to library expenditures, acquisitions procedures, library policies, and available services. At the same time, librarians needed to learn more about department's curricular needs and future endeavors in order to suggest worthwhile services and solicit collection development suggestions.

In response to these needs, the working group developed library liaison "toolkits." These toolkits referred to two complementary resources: first, a physical toolkit of library and college-related information; second, a series of in-house training sessions that addressed library policies and effective communication.

THE PHYSICAL TOOLKIT

A number of potentially useful resources were collected and distributed to liaisons. These materials included

- The College Factbook (an annual statistical snapshot of the college).
- The schedule of classes and course catalogs.
- College phone and e-mail directory.
- Lists of new faculty. These were supplied through departments themselves, or through the Human Resources office.
- Library Annual Reports.
- College press releases and newsletters. These are generally an effective way to find out about new faculty publications, grants, and changes in academic programs.
- Library brochures, newsletters, and other promotional materials. Working with these tools gave the library an opportunity to review and revise its marketing materials.
- List of subscriptions and recent expenditures.
- The library's Website. For many liaisons, the Website was an excellent resource for developing discipline-specific electronic pathfinders.
- Library policies and services. It became clear early in the program that librarians needed a centralized repository for information about

the library, e.g., circulation and reserves policies. In order to facilitate access to this information, an effort was made to post services on the library's Website.

- Working knowledge of general and discipline-specific tools. While many liaisons had daily contact with electronic and print research tools, an effort was made to ensure that all liaisons were able to perform high-level OPAC and database functions, e.g., placing holds on books, manipulating full-text articles.

- Other, optional skills. These included desktop publishing software access and assistance in generating acquisitions expenditures reports.

Many of these skills were addressed by in-house experts, based upon individual needs.

TOOLKIT SESSIONS

LLWG members developed a series of workshops that highlighted library services and communication skills. Each was about one hour in length and incorporated demonstrations (e.g., from databases and acquisitions system) PowerPoint®-enhanced discussions, and hands-on exercises. Attendance was voluntary, and was open to the entire library staff.

One Toolkit session, "Learning about a Department," featured parts of the physical toolkit, including student demographic information, notices of new appointments and retirements, and campus newsletters. All of these provide the liaison with insights into new developments in their departments. (See Figure 5 for an excerpt.)

Another toolkit session focused on the importance of making referrals to other departments. Many potential liaisons were apprehensive about being able to answer complex questions about library services, especially those in which they were not local experts. The toolkit session was designed to highlight the importance of making referrals confidently and of trusting one's co-workers to handle referred queries professionally. (See Figure 6 for an excerpt.)

Another toolkit session provided an overview of the complex acquisitions process. At New Paltz, funds for monographs, journals, etc., are neither absolute dollar figures nor are they determined by formula. Additionally, the library itself is traditionally responsible for selection and,

FIGURE 5. Liaison Toolkit Session, "Learning About a Department" Excerpt

Building a Relationship

- with the department and with individuals
- working toward a common goal, i.e., student learning, faculty research
- helping faculty achieve their objectives
- developing a partnership

What Faculty Want in a Librarian . . . **(based on Stahl, 1997)**

- "Proactivity is the first trait I want . . . tempered with an acute sense of when to back off."
- "Clear communication."
- "Prefer directness over grudging acquiescence."
- "Inform and keep informing me."
- "I need reminding again and again and again."
- "How can I contribute to building the library?"
- "Your excitement over a new resource sparks my interest."
- Subject mastery is not required, but a basic understanding is important.

Find Out

- What the department does
- What the faculty does

How to Find Out

- department Web page
- faculty Web pages
- course schedule
- faculty interest survey
- College newsletters and press releases
- local newspapers
- e-mail/print announcements and invitations

Let Them Know About You

- your knowledge (or not) of their discipline
- how you were paired with the department
- your role at STL

How to Connect

- Director will contact deans and chairs first
- Liaison should meet with chair separately
- Meet the secretary

Keep It Simple

- Don't promise more than you can deliver.
- Be responsive.
- Follow through.
- Remember that you have support.

FIGURE 6. Liaison Toolkit Session, "Making Referrals" Excerpt

The Reference Librarian is an intermediary, ombudsman, and troubleshooter. . . often between patrons and the library's many departments.

–Jennerich and Jennerich (1987, 78)

There are areas where you already refer patrons:

- Patron needs an item being cataloged or out for repair
- Discrepancies in the catalog
- Mediated searching
- Confused by the building
- Fines, checkout questions
- Patron is upset/has complaints about facilities or technology

Academic Advisors make referrals all the time:

- Advisors have the responsibility to know all available campus resources.
- Advisors need to listen carefully to students, in order to pinpoint the best resources.

Making a good referral–Honesty, Confidence, Follow-up
Self-education and awareness are very helpful. **Learn what your colleagues do!**

- STL Webpage
- Library policies and forms
- Workshops, brown bags
- Networking

Referring, or being referred to by someone, shows trust and confidence in the library's relationship with the faculty member–not that you are the next bureaucrat up the chain of command.

Conclusions
When making a referral, it is important to remember:

- Making a referral is good reference work.
- Your referral is a sign of confidence. You are not letting this person down, or letting yourself off the hook.
- Your referral means you have an interest in the outcome. Follow-up with the faculty person or the person to whom they've been referred. The method is your choice: e-mail or voice mail, a quick coffee, a scheduled meeting . . .
- The person that you are referring will probably return for future transactions. You are a source of information, even though you don't have all the answers. "Give a referral, get a referral!"
- Keep apprised of library and campus happenings.

ultimately, purchasing (unlike many institutions, where the academic departments are charged with expending their own funds). Given this situation–and the fact that many classroom instructors had not made many acquisitions selections–it was imperative that liaisons have a solid understanding of the acquisitions process, and that they could communicate these processes to inquiring faculty in jargon-free terms.

Handouts and multimedia from the toolkit sessions were archived on the in-house LAN should liaisons desire them. To date, several newer liaisons have reported their usefulness as instructional tools.

OUTREACH ENDEAVORS

In order to jumpstart the outreach initiative, the library director sent letters to deans and department chairs regarding the pilot program. These were followed with promotional flyers sent to individual faculty members. Liaisons were encouraged to follow-up with departments at a level they felt comfortable; some elected to communicate by phone or e-mail, while others secured invitations to departmental meetings.

From the outset, liaisons were encouraged to explore diverse means of communication and to participate in faculty collaboration at a level that was comfortable for them. Some notable activities have included:

- Acting as referral agent between instructors and various library departments
- Creating e-mails, newsletters, and brochures to announce new services and to encourage faculty participation in collection development
- Observing classroom faculty during lectures
- Attending departmental meetings and department-sponsored events
- Initiating database trials
- Hosting library orientation sessions for new faculty
- Communicating with departments during serials review initiatives
- Developing and teaching library instruction sessions
- Providing customized research consultations to faculty and students
- Team-teaching and syllabus development

POSTSCRIPT: PROGRAM ASSESSMENT

Two years into this initiative, the library liaison working group, in cooperation with the liaisons and the library director, are beginning to devise methods to assess the quality of the program.

We can look at the assessment of the liaison program from two perspectives. First, is there a discernable increase in faculty participation in collection development and other library endeavors? Or, tangentially, do the faculty feel better about the library as a whole? Do they feel more aware of our services, and do they have a greater sense that they can use the library effectively and recommend its services to others? Secondly, we can address assessment from the perspective of the liaison: Do the liaisons feel they are doing an adequate job, that they see the results of their outreach endeavors bearing fruit (e.g., in the form of increased communication, referrals from faculty)?

In general, there appears to be an increased interest in collection development among departments who have a liaison. Many liaisons report increased feedback and questions about the library from their faculties. In addition, many services that the liaisons promote, such as electronic reserves and library instruction, have increased. But in general, it is a challenge to discern the impact of liaison communication upon these developments in library services.

We are just as curious about the individuals–and occasionally, whole departments–who do not acknowledge liaison's promotional endeavors. Have we changed their opinions about the library, or enlightened them as to new services? Do they refer others to our services, despite being tacit themselves?

In the latter case, many liaisons report a feeling of accomplishment and personal reward. In a recent survey of the liaisons, several responses singled out new relationships with teaching faculty, and a palpable sense of "partnership" with classroom instructors as being especially rewarding. Others report that their assigned departments rarely acknowledge their promotional initiatives. It is admittedly difficult to qualify success based upon impromptu meetings, occasional phone calls and e-mails, and the like.

While still in the planning stages, the library is considering a number of approaches in order to assess the program's success. Some of these methods may include faculty surveys and focus groups, an analysis of which departments use which library services, a longitudinal examination of faculty purchase requests, and interviewing liaisons to gain a deeper perspective on their communication experiences in order to develop best practices.

REFERENCES

Dilmore, Donald H. 1996. Librarian/faculty interaction at nine New England colleges. *College & Research Libraries* 57: 274-284.

Fyffe, Richard C. and Paul J. Kobulnicky. 1999. Negotiating the soul of the library: Change management in information access and local collection development. *Journal of Library Administration* 28: 4: 17-35.

Jakubs, Deborah. 1999. Staffing for collection development in the electronic environment: Toward a new definition of roles and responsibilities. *Journal of Library Administration* 28: 4: 71-83.

Jennerich, Elaine Z., and Edward J. Jennerich. 1987. *The reference interview as a creative art.* Littleton, CO: Libraries Unlimited.

Mozenter, Frada, Bridgette T. Sanders, and Jeanie M. Welch. 2000. Restructuring a liaison program in an academic library. *College & Research Libraries* 61: 5: 432-439.

Phipps, Shelley. 2001. Beyond measuring service quality: Learning from the voices of the customers, the staff, the processes, and the organization. *Library Trends* 49: 4: 635-661.

Ray, Ron L. 1998. Where is the future of acquisitions expertise written in the future of libraries? *Journal of Library Administration* 24 (1): 80-82.

Stahl, Aletha D. 1997. "What I want in a librarian: One new faculty member's perspective. *Reference & User Services Quarterly* 37 (2): 133-135.

Stoffle, Carla J., Janet Fore, and Barbara Allen. 1999. Developing new models for collection development. *Journal of Library Administration* 28: 4: 3-15.

Wu, Connie, Michael Bowman, Judy Gardner, Robert G. Sewell, and Myoung Chung Wilson. 1994. Effective liaison relationships in an academic library. *C&RL News* 55: 5: 254, 301.

Index

Page numbers in *italics* indicate figures; page numbers followed by "t" indicate tables.